JUSTIN VIVIAN BOND

TANGO

My Childhood, Backwards and in High Heels

PREFACE BY HILTON ALS

fp

**THE
FEMINIST PRESS**
AT THE CITY UNIVERSITY
OF NEW YORK
NEW YORK CITY

Published in 2011 by the Feminist Press
at the City University of New York
The Graduate Center
365 Fifth Avenue, Suite 5406
New York, NY 10016

feministpress.org

First printing September 2011

Cover design by Herb Thornby, herbthornby.com
Cover photo by David Kimelman
Text design by Drew Stevens

Library of Congress Cataloging-in-Publication Data

Bond, Justin.
 Tango : my childhood, backwards and in high heels / by Justin Vivian Bond.
    p. cm.
 ISBN 978-1-55861-747-6
 1. Bond, Justin. 2. Singers—United States—Biography. I. Title.
 ML420.B6846A3 2011
 792.7092—dc22
 [B]

                                                         2011011372

Preface
BY HILTON ALS

A LONG TIME AGO, I USED TO SPEND TIME WITH
the members of a dance troupe; they performed
under the name Tango Argentina, and, once or
twice a week, I went to see them perform; their
dance of passion—the tango—was an early twen-
tieth-century invention, and had been culled,
shaped, out of the music and dancing style poor
blacks brought with them from Africa to places
like Buenos Aires and Montevideo; the tango
dancers I knew on Broadway, performing night
after night in front of an enthralled audience,
followed the spectacle's attitudinal rules; that is,
the men danced in a way that was meant to exag-
gerate their maleness as they moved about the
stage in dark suits, while the women accentu-

ated their femaleness in heels that made their ankles wobble; in short, I learned, fairly quickly, that the tango was gender-based; men lead the women but the women controlled the rhythm of the couple's movements with a shift of the hips, a turning away of the head; the women contributed greatly to this moving picture of love gone awry by projecting their powerful difference and anger while drawing the men into their interior world; all that aside, I loved looking at those doomed-seeming partners as they moved through that abstraction known as dance; it was like watching a sentence unravel; or sometimes I imagined the dancers' sinuous moves as the visualization of breathing itself, breath as it moved in and out of the body, providing sustenance to the dancers, or maybe not even the dancers, maybe just you in your darkened bedroom, wondering if your body would mean as much to someone in the world as those dancers meant to an audience sitting in the dark, one that maybe took a look at the history of their respective bodies as the dancers moved across that stage, sometimes inciting audience members to wonder about their own bodies, and how, as men and women living strictly in maleness and femaleness, they had limited their movements let alone their lives, in order to fit categorizations or stock characters that fill the world stage, wherever that is; and I probably wouldn't have remembered my friends over at Tango Argentina—time erases us all—had I not read Mx Justin Vivian Bond's book, *Tango*, which hardly needs an introduction, but I am very grateful for the opportunity to write this sentence nevertheless, or have this exhalation of breath, if only to say I can relax now, Justin Vivian has, finally, talked about bodies in a way all of us can understand, bodies moving in space, specifically Mx's own, and through sentences that cause my body to stop wondering what it might mean to others while starting to wonder what this mortal coil might mean to myself, in the dark or in the light, held by my own hands, or the hands of others; in *Tango* and elsewhere, the performer and singer Justin Vivian has learned to dance with V's self, to wear the heels and the suit that fit V's being, all cut and formed to suit V's soul, having earned it as so many of us earn it, through being brutalized and suppressed and sometimes through love, too; this sentence could go on; it could go on to talk about Justin Vivian's authorial voice, which tells us, in so many words, about being Mx from the beginning, and then being told not to be, except in the safe home of a man who kissed his dead wife's picture every night before he went to bed; and I wondered, while reading *Tango*, what that might have meant to little Mx, seeing the dead image of a dead woman and bringing pleasure to an old man who liked Mx's Ginger as much as Mx's Fred; and I wonder, too, about the boulder that was removed in Justin Vivian's town so children wouldn't get hurt on it, the antisepticizing impulse of people who don't want to deal with pain and regret even as they inflict it; and, yes, Justin Vivian describes that, too, how the children in his town learned to hurt each other anyway, based on what they learned at home, along with learning to fear their bodies, and the vulnerability that comes with love; and I wondered, too, what darkness looked like in Justin Vivian's room as Mx became Justin Vivian more and more, despite the promulgating of souls all around; did Justin Vivian tango with Mx's own soul in that darkened room as it filled up with a kind of loneliness, and the town filled up with loneliness, too, as Justin Vivian's mother's manifested itself in making her own child an accessory to be dropped at will because love sometimes crushed her, too, and alienated her from her purer impulse, which was to see and celebrate what she saw of herself in Justin Vivian even as she said, No, you must not, you cannot, sport the lipstick I wear, our lips must not touch our shared truths and love of cosmetics, even as I wonder what Justin Vivian's first brush of lipstick smelled like in that riot of closeness and distance called V's family home; even as I imagine, from the pages of this book, what Justin Vivian's tango of the self looked like as Mx grew up to inhabit Justin Vivian's very own passion play on a stage Mx now controls, in a safe arena Mx now makes dangerous, ankles wobbling in high heels, defiantly and naturally sporting a red mouth that pulses like a wound.

"Hey, Fred! Where's Ginger?" my grandfather would ask me. I was always dancing around the house as a child. I didn't know who Fred was, or Ginger for that matter. All I knew was that I liked to dance. After seeing *Top Hat*, I was flattered by the comparison, but I was also confused. Couldn't I be both Fred *and* Ginger?

A FAMOUS COMEDIAN ONCE SAID, THE GREATEST thing about being bisexual is that it doubles your chances for a date on a Saturday night. That might be true, but for me it doubles the anxiety.

Decision making of all kinds has been complicated for me. For instance, deciding on an outfit for a night out on the town isn't easy because I don't buy into the notion of male, female, or age-appropriate clothing, and I don't make a distinction between formal, casual, and sportswear. I can spend hours trying to get in touch with what form of expression my wardrobe choice should take. Sometimes I won't leave the house until three or four in the afternoon because I can't decide if I want to wear eyeliner or not.

Perhaps this indecision comes from feeling like my choices were under so much scrutiny as a child. Certain people have basic tenets or rules. My friend Nancy's mother always said to her, "Never leave the house without your eyebrows." I am not aware of my own mother ever leaving ours without her lipstick. Lipstick is one of the most magical inventions ever created as far as I'm concerned. Generally when I'm talking to a person, I don't look into their eyes, I look into their mouth. The eyes may be the windows into the soul, but the mouth quite often reveals a greater truth.

Iced Watermelon by Revlon, a frosted pink lipstick you could buy at most drugstores in the late 1960s, was my mother's color of choice. When I was in first grade, I got into the habit of applying my mother's Iced Watermelon lipstick before I set off for school. I don't know how many days I got away with it, but I do know that I felt confident when I walked out the door. Knowing that my lipstick was in place, I could safely face the world, having enhanced my beauty with a color that my mother, who was clearly a beautiful woman as well, had chosen. If given the chance, would I have chosen a different color, a hue more unique and self-revelatory? I'll never know. I didn't have my own income at that time or transportation to the drugstore. I made do with what was at hand.

I don't recall anyone at school having a problem with my lipstick. My teacher, Mrs. Bivens, never said anything. Mrs. Bivens had her own glamour rituals. Every morning I looked forward to seeing Mrs. Bivens lead the pledge of allegiance in her high-heeled shoes. I recall blue leather, a standard shoe for a Republican woman and yet, by modern standards, a bit of an extravagant choice considering the only people who saw her in them were a class full of six-year-olds. And yet she displayed a commitment to her self-image and what she clearly thought was appropriate attire. After lunch, when we returned from recess, Mrs. Bivens usually slipped into a sensible flat. This was her ritual and she practiced it every day like clockwork.

We all need rituals. I decided that putting on lipstick would be one of mine. I don't know how many days passed, how many carefree days, walking the block and a half to Pangborn Elementary School like a movie star or a morning television star. We didn't have a color TV at home, but I could tell even from the small black-and-white set that sat on our kitchen counter that Barbara Walters, co-hostess of the *Today Show*, was wearing frosted lipstick. So I left the house, an intrepid reporter like Barbara, who had interviewed Fidel Castro, ready to face any tyrant with confidence. Any tyrant but my mother, who one morning intercepted me as I was about to leave the house.

"What is on your lips?" she asked me in what I could only register as horror.

I froze in fear, not sure what to say. I opted for what I thought at the time was the truth.

"It's my lipstick."

"That's not your lipstick! That's my lipstick. What are you doing with that lipstick on your face?"

"Well, I'm going to school. You don't leave the house without your lipstick, so I thought I should wear lipstick, too."

"Boys don't wear lipstick!" she shouted, as if this were something I should know, and using that word "boy" which grated against the very fiber of my being every time it was applied to me.

"But Mom! I've been wearing it every day. No one cares."

"You've been wearing lipstick to school for days? How many days?"

"I don't know." I was crying. "But it's okay!"

"No, it's not."

She marched me to the bathroom and wiped it off my lips. I left for school that day defeated, disappointed, and bland. It would take me another twenty years before I realized that it was okay to leave the house with my lipstick.

Now that I'm in my forties, frosted pink seems a little too coquettish for a person of my stature. But looking back, I think that frosted pink is a perfect color for a little trans child in first grade. At that time I certainly wasn't allowed to think of myself as a trans child, much less decide what color lipstick was appropriate for one. So many of my thoughts and feelings and ideas became fractured when I was young. So much second-guessing informed every decision that I made that I became a paradox in a way, a combination of bravado and insecurity. The scrutiny I was under by the vigilant gender police kept me aware that my first choice should always be followed by a second or third choice before any decision was ever made. That way of thinking permeated my life and has kept me from moving quickly on any impulse for most of it.

RECENTLY, AT THE AGE OF FORTY-SIX, I WAS scheduled to do a series of performances at the

Sydney Opera House. In preparation for my trip, I asked a friend of mine for some Ambien for the horrible jet lag I anticipated having after the twenty-four-hour journey. He threw in a few Adderall, which he told me would help me wake up and give me energy during the day. I've never really been one for uppers—too many of my friends went crazy in the '90s on crystal meth so I've always shied away from stimulants. But one night, I was expected at a dinner party. Since I was tired and a bit anxious I decided to give the Adderall a try just to see what would happen. I found myself much calmer, and focused.

I was raised that if you have a headache you wait awhile to see if it goes away before you take an aspirin. You only go to the doctor when you are very sick, and you don't buy new shoes until you've worn out the old ones. So even though I felt better on Adderall, I wasn't sure what I should do about it.

A week later, I was at a party speaking with a friend's father, who happened to be a psychologist. He told me I should be careful of Adderall because it is an addictive drug and should only be taken when prescribed. He asked me how it affected me. I explained that my usual dithering was diminished. If I felt sleepy, I knew I should take a nap. If it was time for me to go somewhere, I found myself getting dressed and leaving the hotel. These simple things that most people take for granted became less and less difficult for me. After I described my reactions he said, "You probably have ADD."

Attention deficit disorder. It sounds so strange. A deficit *and* a disorder. Is that like anorexia nervosa? People don't think they have that. Or what's it called when people can't read or write in the right order? Dyslexia! Cher has dyslexia. So does Tom Cruise. They bonded over this condition during their affair in the 1980s. After Cher broke up with Tom, she hooked up with Rob Camilletti, the Bagel Boy. Is my attention deficit disorder causing me to ruminate about tabloid stories of yore right now instead of telling you what sort of confusion the very idea of having ADD stirred up in me?

There was a lot to think about. First of all, if I had ADD it would mean I would have to get a prescription. I hadn't had a prescription for anything other than antibiotics for an occasional strep throat or passing nonspecific urethritis since I was a child. Even then, I didn't have to take anything for an undetermined period of time. Could I afford ADD medication? Perhaps ADD was an affliction to be indulged in by people of a higher economic bracket than mine. Maybe I was just telling my friend's father these things because I wanted to keep taking Adderall. Maybe I was unwittingly becoming a speed freak. Maybe the romance of being like so many of my fallen idols—Judy Garland, Edie Sedgwick, Neely O'Hara—was getting the best of me. God knows I was tired of the show business slog: trying to come up with new acts and the energy to go to new places, the wherewithal to smile at one more stranger . . . Perhaps Adderall or speed or whatever would lighten the load of my incessant and superficial interactions. Conversely, what if Adderall allowed me to focus on all these people, places, and things? Would I get bogged down in the present? Maybe this disorder had served me well over the years. After all, I had managed to carve out a career as a world-class artist to a very boutique audience. They had seen me rise from postage-stamp stages in the back rooms of San Francisco to the legendary Carnegie Hall *twice*, all the while performing as a character who would have been my greatest nightmare to consider as a child. If I'd had Adderall and made informed decisions all my life, where would I be now? Most of my work and strategies in life had been about following my instincts. Having been in Jungian analysis, I had become very comfortable with allowing my unconscious urges and desires to lead the way. Sometimes logic and pragmatism had intercepted my path, but in general I'd never been one to make carefully thought-out and considered decisions.

So when my friend's father said, "You probably have ADD," I was simultaneously relieved and terrified. I knew he was right, and that I would now be required to take action.

First I spoke to the psychoanalyst who I'd been seeing for the past four years. He is one of the few people in my world who I actually think is smarter than me. Although he is suspicious of using medication to offset psychological or mental disquietude, he encouraged me to see a psychiatrist for further exploration.

I made an appointment to go see a doctor. Psychiatrists, I have learned, can be well-educated, compassionate, and caring people, whose main goal is to come up with a quick diagnosis of your psychological infirmity, be it chemical or emotional. Within an hour, the psychiatrist I visited had determined that I do have attention deficit disorder and probably mild depression, and had offered to prescribe medication.

I refused the depression meds because I was suffering from a mild case of heartbreak, having recently broken up with my beloved traveling companion. I had faith that the depression would pass, given some time and some good sex. And it did.

Once I had my prescription I began to reevaluate my past through the lens of this recent discovery. I started remembering what life had been like for me when I was a child. For the first three years of elementary school my desk was always separate from the rest of the class. There were twenty-five students and the teacher, and I was by myself off to the left. I thought this was normal. I wasn't hyperactive or difficult; I think I was just extremely aware of everything going on around me and it was difficult for me to choose which thing to concentrate on the most.

I told my mother of my diagnosis. She seemed surprised and didn't remember the many times she had come in to school on Parents' Day and wondered why I was seated separate from the class. But mothers remember what they want.

A few days later when I was on the phone with my sister Carol, she told me she'd had a conversation with our mom about my ADD. Then she said to me, "Don't you think you were seated separate from the rest of the class because you were always trying to be the center of attention?"

This made me feel like my brain was splitting open. When asked these kinds of loaded questions by my family members, I immediately go on the defensive. I was hurt at the insensitivity of what seemed like her invalidation of what I was telling her, as if my issues were "all in my head." So many things that I felt, thought, or experienced as a child were attributed by my family to being all in my head. When they said something hurtful and I got upset, it was all in my head. When I felt like someone was making fun of me, it was all in my head. If my mother criticized me and I reacted negatively or defensively, I was too sensitive. If I was nervous or upset about something like a performance or show I was about to do, my father would say to me, "Why are you nervous? You have no reason to be nervous."

For a huge portion of my life one of my greatest challenges has been to flatline myself emotionally around my family, because when I expressed my feelings I was told that I was either overreacting or being hysterical. Maybe this was because I bottled so much up that when feelings finally did come through it was in the form of an explosion. Nevertheless, my sister Carol and my mother believed that I was always trying to be the center of attention, and this simply wasn't true.

"No, actually, I think I was made uncomfortable by the fact that I received *too much* attention." My sister didn't seem to believe me.

"It's okay to want a lot of attention. I did. Everyone wants a lot of attention."

"Maybe you wanted a lot of attention. Perhaps that's why you were the president of your class from sixth grade till the end of high school and were voted most popular in your class. I don't think I would have spent most of my teenage years hiding out in my best girlfriend's room reading gothic romance novels and listening to Elton John records if I wanted so much attention."

THE FIRST TIME I WAS SEPARATED FROM THE class was in first grade. I think I felt very lonely then because I wasn't sure exactly where I fit in. Generally, I found myself befriending the less outgoing, shy people in the class. I was very good at bringing them out of their shells and making them laugh. I was attracted to outsiders. I always felt very skittish when surrounded by too many people—when I felt like I had too many eyes upon me.

I have a cousin Pam who's three months younger than I and who I always felt extremely close to. When I wasn't with her I imagined she was with me, and I took great comfort in her presence. I distinctly recall arranging it so that I had to sit at the end of the row of desks in order that there would be room for a desk for my invisible cousin to sit next to me. There was an imaginary desk for an imaginary friend in an open space, which made me feel safe. I quickly learned that if

I got stuck between two people all I had to do was engage them in too much conversation and my desk would be moved. I would be seated on my own and have a space to create a world around me where I felt safe, in spite of the fact that I had a "behavioral problem." When on my own I was perfectly fine. When left to myself without the distractions of so many people around me I was much better able to focus on the tasks at hand. I realize now that my "need for attention" was really more of a need for simplicity.

I STARTED ELEMENTARY SCHOOL IN 1969. AT THAT time, people weren't diagnosing children with mental health issues the way that they do today. We were just "trouble." I mention this because Carol, during the same recent conversation, told me a story about a boy who grew up next door to us who had been my archnemesis and who had recently been arrested for impersonating a drug enforcement agent out on Route 81. Evidently they had nabbed him somewhere between the Valley Mall and Martinsburg, West Virginia.

According to my sister he had been operating under an assumed code name: Tango.

"Did you hear about Michael Hunter?"

Immediately I felt a fluttering in my stomach. I hadn't seen Michael Hunter anywhere other than in my dreams for a good long time. In spite of the fact that I hated him, we had been lovers, if you could call it that, from the ages of eleven to sixteen. My sister knew there had been a lot of tension between us when we were kids, but I don't know if she really knew the full extent of our relationship. Nonetheless we got a good laugh that he had given himself the code name "Tango," and wondered if it came from the 1980s Kurt Russell movie *Tango and Cash* in which Kurt Russell plays a narcotics detective who is paired up with a partner he can't stand but with whom he has to work in order to clear his name. Clearly, Michael Hunter was living a life of delusion and may have had some kind of psychotic break.

It is a terrible thing to laugh at another's misfortunes, but Carol and I couldn't help but laugh at the absurdities of Michael Hunter's arrest that day. As soon as I got off the phone, I went online and found a newspaper article about his arrest with the headline "Man Posing as Cop Nabbed," along with his mug shot. His face looked tragic. He had become a middle-aged bald man. Instead of feeling any kind of satisfaction I felt tremendous sadness because I knew that he had been through hell. I did think, however, that calling himself Tango showed that somewhere inside he still had a touch of panache. I thought of Kurt Russell who had gone from playing a boy who could make himself invisible in Disney's *Now You See Him, Now You Don't* to being a gun-toting action adventure hero in such films as *Escape from New York* and *Death Proof*. The newspaper said that Tango was wearing a bullet-proof vest, fatigues, and a green shirt that read JOINT TERRORIST TASK FORCE when he was arrested. He probably thought he was starring in *Death Proof 2: The Sequel.*

It was reported that the police had found handcuffs, two-way radios, and various law enforcement equipment in Michael's blue BMW. Reading this, many memories came flooding back. This definitely wasn't the first time "Tango" had impersonated a law officer. Tango and I had a history of arrest ourselves. When we were young, one of the games we liked to play involved one of us posing as an undercover police officer and the other as a criminal. Many summer afternoons were spent getting frisked in his parents' two-car garage, where invariably one of us was found with a concealed weapon in his pants.

It was all too much. After reading the article I called my sister back. Carol is now an elementary school vice principal who deals with lots of medicated children. Looking back, we both agreed that Michael had probably had mental health issues since childhood.

"YOU WALK LIKE A GIRL."

"No, I don't."

"Yes, you do. You walk like a girl."

"Well, I'm a boy, and this is how I walk. So I don't walk like a girl, I walk like a boy."

I had this conversation with a little girl when I was nine years old, in the fourth grade. I remember the spot where it happened. It was in the doorway at Pangborn Boulevard Elementary School as we were exiting onto the playground. She didn't say it to be rude. It was just an observation. For me, it was more complex. I was simultaneously flattered and confused. I hadn't been aware that I walked like a girl. I don't even know that I aspired to walk like a girl. But I'm sure I never tried to walk like a boy. I didn't like boys. I'd never really liked boys.

FOR THE FIRST PART OF MY LIFE, I THINK MY role was very clearly defined: I was my mother's most glamorous accessory. I was cute, fairly at ease socially, and I began talking at a very young age. My parents were delighted that their first child was a boy and it was several more years until my sister came along, so I was the focus of quite a lot of attention.

I was mostly surrounded by women and girls. My mother's best friend, who I called Aunt Judy, had a daughter who was one year older than me. I had a girl cousin who was three months younger than me and a slew of female teenage cousins who were always dropping by, especially when they needed to use our bathroom as they were headed from their house in the country to go shopping downtown.

I was raised by girls and I liked it. I was like a pet monkey that they would tease and dress up and play with. This seemed perfectly normal to me and I remember enjoying it. Once I entered school in the autumn of 1969, I was thrown into social situations with boys for the first time. I was appalled. They were always racing around, screaming loudly, playing with trucks, throwing balls, wrestling, and sweating. I found it disgusting and unnerving. I wasn't used to so much aggression and commotion. I preferred skipping rope and playing house to running around. I enjoyed climbing the jungle gym with the girls. My teachers' reports were always the same: "He is very alert, a good student, but needs to learn how to play with the other boys."

By the time fourth grade rolled around, I had become fairly comfortable with most of the boys in my class simply because I was familiar with them, as it was a small school. Nonetheless, I didn't play or socialize with them. I'd had several girlfriends, and as a matter of fact I had "married" Patty Chase in second grade. Her sister performed the ceremony in her parents' house, and I was devastated when I was told we weren't going to be allowed to live together. Obviously, when no one took our marriage seriously, I became disillusioned. Well, they had their chance . . . Anyway, I had several girlfriends in the fourth grade, including Kim Bell who wore white go-go boots to school. I was very happy because I got to sit next to her and stroke her go-go boots, which to me had the texture of marshmallow fluff, one of my favorite treats. Kim didn't seem to mind me stroking her go-go boots one bit, and my teacher didn't stop me because I think she was relieved that I was showing interest in a girl instead of trying to be one.

IN 1964, MY PARENTS BOUGHT A THREE-BEDROOM ranch house in a development at the edge of town. Our street was paved, but the rest of the freshly plowed area consisted of red clay. The Kendalls, our neighbors to the rear, had a son named Greg who was a bit younger than me, and I quickly became friends with him. In their front yard they had a great big boulder that we used to play on, until someone fell and scraped their knee and the boulder had to be removed. That's how it was then. They tried to keep us from climbing trees in case we fell out. They removed boulders so no one would skin their knees. I'm surprised they didn't put cotton bunting on the sidewalk in case someone fell. It was all about the safety of the children.

Next to the Kendalls, a new house was being built. Eventually, a couple moved in with their daughter, Eva. They had an aboveground pool, which was very exotic, and they were almost, but not quite, hippies. The Brinings were young and cool and much hipper than anyone else in the neighborhood. Eva became one of our best friends. Greg, Eva, and I played together every day. But one day when we knocked on her door, her father said that Eva wasn't living there anymore. Our parents told us that she wouldn't be coming back because her parents were getting a divorce. This was the first time anyone we knew had parents who got divorced, and it was sad for us because our friend just disappeared.

THE BRININGS' HOUSE WAS SOLD TO AN AFRICAN American man named Mr. White. Mr. White was a bachelor and the first African American man to move into our neighborhood. We were very excited and wanted to welcome our new neighbor. We didn't know how to make a pie and our mothers were busy so we decided that since we had just gotten a new set of crayons, and since he was a "colored" man, Greg and I would write him a poem using all of our new colors: *Red is nice, we like red. Green is nice, we like green . . .* making our way through all of the colors . . . *we like purple, blue . . . we LOVE White!* Then we got to black. *Black is ugly, we hate black.*

Very excited and proud of our poem, we knocked on Mr. White's door, smiling from ear to ear, and handed it to him. We said, "Welcome to our neighborhood, Mr. White!" He looked at the card. We were sure he would be delighted by our neighborliness but instead he looked very shocked and asked, "Do your parents know you wrote this?"

"No. We did it on our own, Mr. White. We would have baked a pie but we don't know how."

He didn't seem at all pleased with our gift, which was very confusing to us. We went home and told our parents Mr. White wasn't very friendly. Soon, they received a phone call from Mr. White and we got into big trouble. We hadn't realized Mr. White was black, we thought he was colored, which is why we wrote him a poem about all the colors we liked. Most kids prefer red or green to black, but we didn't realize that saying we hated black would be an insult to Mr. White. Our parents brought us over to his house and, in tears, we apologized. "We're so sorry Mr. White. We didn't know you were black."

He was very nice to us from then on, although he moved out a few years later. In all honesty we were glad he moved out because we wanted someone fun like Eva to move back in there. And Mr. White didn't let us swim in his pool.

FINALLY, A NEW FAMILY MOVED IN. THE HUNT-
ers. They had two boys, one of whom was my
age, named Michael, and his older brother,
named Bobby. On Michael's first day of school I
discovered he was in my class at Pangborn and
our teacher Mrs. Schmid, clearly with an agenda,
decided I should show Michael around since he
was my new neighbor. I was very interested in
knowing what Michael was like but I was also
suspicious of the motives of adults, and I quickly
realized this was her attempt to find me a boy
friend.

I thought, I'll give this Michael boy a chance.
He talked about how he had lived in a very nice
neighborhood in New Jersey, much nicer than
the one we lived in, and told me that his father's
company had provided all the glass for the new
United Nations building. I thought to myself,
"This boy's full of crap, and I have to take him
down a notch." He was very full of himself and
clearly was seeking to impress. I approached
relations with most boys with an air of studied
disdain, but Michael Hunter had my hackles up
immediately. I was unaware that the UN building

had been erected in 1952 but I knew well enough not to believe him. I didn't come straight out and call him a liar, but he could tell that I knew he was full of it.

One thing I was pretty sure I knew how to do was to be condescending to men and boys. Having three teenage cousins during the era of women's lib had taught me quite a bit about sarcasm and just how far a good roll of the eyes could take you. These were the times when you couldn't turn on the TV without a news report making reference to the women's movement, *Roe v. Wade*, and the fight for the Equal Rights Amendment. Gloria Steinem was on with her frosted hair and wire-frame glasses, and Bea Arthur was starring in a sitcom called *Maude* in which her famous line was "God'll get you for that, Walter," which not only put her husband Walter in his place, but God in hers. My greatest role model on television was Cher. *The Sonny and Cher Show* always had a segment where Cher would one-up Sunny with her put-downs.

Any chance I got to show my finely honed skills at bitchiness was okay by me. I didn't really think of it as being mean, I thought of it as having fun. Michael Hunter might have thought otherwise. I can't remember what I said to him that first day in school, but I know I made him feel like shit. By the end of the day, I had definitely not made a new friend. Nonetheless, I had begun one of the most intense relationships of my early years.

In many ways, Michael was everything that I was not. Brash, confident, athletic, and charming in a guileless, almost needy, sort of way. He had brown hair, which got much lighter in the summer, brown eyes, thick eyebrows for a kid, and one unusual feature that we all noticed immediately: the last section of his index finger had been reattached. I forget how he lost his finger, and even if he told me it was probably a lie. I always said his mouth ran so fast he probably bit it off himself.

AT THE TIME MICHAEL MOVED INTO THE NEIGH-borhood I was extremely active in the Cub Scouts of America. It was one of the only activities that my parents got me involved in that I enjoyed. I liked dressing up in the uniform, and there were lots of activities that I thought were fun: hiking, camping, and yearly Pinewood Derby races. My father and I would work together to make my Pinewood Derby car. I remember the first year I wanted my car to look like a Corvette Stingray and we carved the aerodynamic model car out of a kit. I also got to choose the color, which was a kind of metallic green that I had seen on Liza Minnelli's fingernails when I watched a little part of *Cabaret* on TV one night. I was sent to bed shortly after the movie began, but not before I had time to clock those nails.

I never really have thought of myself as a competitive person, but with that first Pinewood Derby race I realized I liked winning. The car was allowed a certain weight, and in order to achieve that weight my father carved a ridge inside the car and melted lead into the front before gluing it back together. My car took the lead immediately and I won the race and was presented with a huge trophy, which still hangs from the ceiling in my parents' basement. The next year, when I was trying to come up with an idea for what I wanted my car to look like, I took my inspiration from a Warner Brothers cartoon and we carved it to look like one of Bugs Bunny's carrots.

My best friend at the time was a boy named Jay Floyd, who lived down the street. I made his mother very nervous. She was a kindergarten teacher at our school and I had always been a very outspoken, some might even say sassy, child. As I mentioned earlier, this was the era of women's lib, and I always liked seeing news reports of feminists on TV marching for women's rights, burning their bras, carrying signs, and asserting that both genders were equal. Somehow, in my mind, I'd come up with the theory that if men and women were equal, it wouldn't matter if I was a man or a woman. I made a sign that read *Kids Lib!* and started carrying it around the neighborhood. If men and women were equal, then kids should be equal too. My friend's mother didn't agree with my philosophy at all. She said children weren't supposed to be liberated, they were supposed to listen to their parents, and she sent me home and told me never to come over with that sign again.

Jay used to take me into his father's workroom where I saw lots of great big pictures of his mother that his father, evidently an amateur photographer, had taken. She was in lingerie posed seductively in front of the fireplace. Ordinarily, this would have seemed like a very exciting, glamorous thing because I loved looking at the photos in the lingerie section of the Sears catalog. They were the only pictures I could find of women posing in gowns like the ones I saw on TV. I used to sit and draw gowns, imagining how one day when I got older and my boobs came in, I would design my own. But Janice Floyd looked nothing like Cher, believe me, so I thought the pictures were creepy. Jay had two older brothers who played rock-and-roll music. One of them worked at McDonald's, which made him very cool in my eyes because he would bring Happy Meals home. Sometimes I would get to stay and eat McDonald's at their house. Unfortunately for Jay, his father was rarely home, so he didn't have much help when it came to making his Pinewood Derby car. The second year I competed in the derby race, Jay's mother was one of the judges. As the race began I was very confident. Because I had won the year before and because the carrot shape of my latest car was even more aerodynamic than the last year's, I was certain that I would be victorious again. I was rooting for Jay because he was my best friend, but obviously I wanted to win. Before the race was even half over, two wheels fell off of Jay's car. My car, my carrot, Bugs Bunny's carrot, wasn't quite as aerodynamic as I had hoped so it didn't shoot out of the gate quite as quickly as my green Corvette Stingray from the year before.

It was a tight race, a very tight race, practically a photo finish. Nonetheless I was sure I had won, but someone else was declared the winner. To this day I swear I heard Janice Floyd whisper into the ear of the other judges, "He won last year; I think we should give it to . . ." and with that my hopes of victory were dashed. I took it personally. Even then, I knew that for people like Janice Floyd, I was a menace to the status quo with my signs, my opinions, and my forbidden knowledge of her lingerie model past. And I couldn't help but feel that she was taking out on me her dissatisfaction with the fact that her husband wasn't there to help her son build a winning car.

I ADMIRED JAY BECAUSE HE WAS SMART, A VERY good piano player, and because he liked to roller skate. He was also the first kid I ever knew who wore glasses.

I wanted to wear glasses because Sandy Duncan, my favorite TV star at the time, wore glasses. Tragically, Sandy Duncan had to leave her number one TV show *Funny Face* on CBS on Saturday nights because she had a brain tumor and had a glass eye put in. I read about her in the movie magazines and I admired her courage and the strength it took to recover from a life-threatening brain operation. After she got out of the hospital there were lots of pictures of her wearing very chic oversize glasses. I wanted glasses too. I wanted to be just like Sandy Duncan and survive a brain tumor so that everyone would know what I was made of.

I read in *Photoplay Magazine* that her hair was auburn, so I took all the money from my piggy bank and bought some auburn hair dye. I was terribly upset when my mother wouldn't let me color my hair. I didn't know why you couldn't dye your hair at seven years old. I thought I would look very good with auburn hair and glasses. But instead of helping me dye my hair, my mother confiscated my color and sent me to my room.

But that didn't stop me from choosing Sandy Duncan as the figure in history whom I would most like to be, at a Cub Scout meeting. The other boys chose to be people like Baltimore Orioles pitcher Jim Palmer, General Robert E. Lee, or John Wayne, but I chose to be Sandy Duncan, a one-eyed pixie who had her own TV show and who was on a TV commercial where she sat in the middle of a wheat field pluckily eating crackers out of a cardboard box!

BY THE TIME MICHAEL HUNTER HAD MOVED INTO the neighborhood I had graduated from being a Cub Scout into a Webelo, which was sort of an older version of a Cub Scout, but not yet a Boy Scout. My mother was the den mother. For some reason, my mother and I did not get along at those Webelo meetings. I don't know if she picked on me excessively or if the way I behaved made it clear to her that I was not like the other boys, but it was not fun. Whatever the reason, I felt like she treated me differently than she did when we were alone and I didn't like it. She was very critical of me and I hadn't experienced that constant criticism from other adults. So what used to be fun for me became a sort of torture.

When Michael Hunter joined our group, he became her pet, or at least that's how it seemed to me. He was an aggressive go-getter and had the chaotic energy of a boy, albeit one who knew how to charm adult women. I knew how to charm adult women too, but my charm lay more in my ability to emulate and match their energy; his charm was more courtly and exasperating.

I didn't like Michael's mother at all—she was loud and mean and not very pretty. When we would play at his house she would yell a lot. I didn't like people who yelled, and I wasn't used to it. My mother didn't yell very much, but she could turn on a dime. Most of the time she was a lot of fun; she could be very silly and affectionate. I loved it when she took me shopping and let me help her pick out her shoes. But there were times when she turned mean, seemingly for no reason, and I couldn't rationalize or explain to myself why. I had a theory that aliens periodically came and stole my real mother and replaced her with this horrible look-alike. After a certain period of time, I became used to the nasty look-alike and would just wait until my loving mother came home.

MICHAEL'S PARENTS SEEMED LIKE ALIENS TO ME. His mother yelled too much and his father kept *Playboy* magazines hidden in their living room, as I discovered one day when Michael and I were horsing around. We knocked the chair over and a *Playboy* slid out from under the cushion. My mother had told me *Playboy* magazines were sinful and exploited women; my dad added that most of the women who were in it were probably drug addicts and had no choice but to pose naked to support their habits.

I thought it was strange that Mr. Hunter kept his *Playboy* magazines in a chair in the living room. It didn't seem like a very good place to hide anything. My Pop-Pop kept his *Playboys* in a three-foot stack next to his easy chair. Pop-Pop was my dad's stepfather. He had married my grandmother, who was twenty-five years his junior, when my father was in his early teens. He moved the family to Hagerstown from the small town that they lived in further west in Maryland near the border of West Virginia. My father's parents divorced when he was three years old, so he was raised by his maternal grandmother, his mother, and his best friend's mother, who was a widow.

My father had no clue what a father's role was supposed to be. Pop-Pop already had a son and wasn't particularly interested in my father, but when I was born, he doted on me, indulging and encouraging all of my artistic endeavors. I never stopped dancing, and I walked on my tiptoes imagining that I was in high heels, which he thought was very funny. He called me "twinkle toes" and we were very close. My cousins on my mother's side told me he was going to go to hell because he hadn't accepted Jesus as his personal lord and savior. Pop-Pop said it was good enough to be nice, which was a lot more than most Christians were. I couldn't argue with that.

Pop-Pop was one of the nicest people I knew even if he had a stack of *Playboys* next to his chair. He took me shopping every week and gave me a dollar to buy anything I wanted. I always bought Barbie coloring books and he didn't bat an eye. I figured if he could buy *Playboy*, I could buy Barbie.

In spite of any comments my mother may have made on the subject, Pop-Pop and I had an understanding. Sometimes my parents would drop me off at his house for him to babysit me, and I can assure you I looked at every single page of every single one of those *Playboy* magazines while Pop-Pop smoked his Tiparillos and drank his Duke Pilsner. The whole house smelled like cigar smoke and nothing had been changed since my grandmother's death from multiple sclerosis a few years before. There were so many pictures of her that you couldn't turn your head without having her look back at you. The glass in front of the portraits had smudge marks over her lips where my grandfather had kissed her good night every night. It was sort of gross, all that lip skin building up over the years, but still it was touching and wildly romantic. Pop-Pop probably thought I was looking through those magazines because I was fascinated by the bunnies. In fact, I was looking to find any little glimpse of a naked man. I couldn't understand how a magazine about sexuality could be so devoid of any representation of commingling but I guessed, knowing how stupid men were, that they would get jealous if someone else was in the picture to interrupt their fantasy.

Having *Playboys* made my grandfather seem cool to me. He was in his eighties and a widower—those Playmates were the only ladies he

had to keep him company. Mr. Hunter, on the other hand, was married. Surely, lusting after those girls in that magazine was disrespectful of his vows to be faithful to his wife. At least that's what I was told. He also had a flattop, which was definitely not in fashion in the early seventies.

AT THE END OF THE FIFTH GRADE, WE GRADU-ated from being Webelos to become Boy Scouts. It was at that time we had to choose which Scout troop we wished to belong to. It seemed that most of the boys who I liked, including my friend Jay, were going to join Troop 34 at the Methodist Church downtown. The Scout leader was my father's doctor. Even though we went to the Church of the Brethren, my father had been raised a Methodist and felt like this would be a good troop for me. I joined. As soon as school got out, I found out we were all going to Boy Scout Camp, which was not something I was particularly excited about. I didn't want to be at a camp for an entire week with just boys.

We all had to have physicals in order to go to Camp Sinoquipe and since our leader was a doctor, we had to stand in line as he sat on a folding chair in the recreational hall of the church and drop our pants in front of him so he could feel our testicles and make sure none of us had hernias. I don't remember him checking for much else (and I don't think this would happen today: the Scout leader fondling the entire troop's balls) and we all passed our physicals and were sent off to camp. I had just turned eleven years old.

On the first day, even before our parents had left, we had to take a swimming test before we would be allowed to swim in the deep part of the lake. We had to swim from the dock to a buoy and back. I had no interest in swimming in the deep part; I just wanted to play in the water close to the shore. I knew how to swim but I was not a confident swimmer, and I didn't want to have to take the test while everyone was looking. My father insisted that I do it. I argued and we had a terrible fight. He threatened to spank me and take me home if I didn't do what he said, so I dove into the cold mountain lake and began to swim.

In June in the mountains, lake water has pockets of warmth and then very frigid areas, so the temperature is constantly changing as you move through it. I got about three-quarters of the way to the buoy and my muscles froze. I started to go under. I was angry and scared, and the lifeguard had to come and fish me out. I was so upset with my father for forcing me to do something that I knew I couldn't do. And to make matters worse, my father was upset with me because his boss's son was the lifeguard who had to rescue me. He'd never live that one down. I was completely embarrassed and knew full well that because it was the first thing the other boys had seen me do, I was in for a rough week. Fortunately Jay was with me and his father wasn't there to force him into the same embarrassing situation so I had someone to play with in the shallow water. By the end of the week I took the swimming test again and I made it with no trouble. Jay did, too.

JAY AND I WERE TENT-MATES. I WAS PEA GREEN with envy because he had pink swimming trunks. I was pretty sure I couldn't get away with pink swimming trunks but because his last name was Floyd, everyone began calling him Pink Floyd and he was immediately cool.

Michael Hunter didn't really have a best friend in the Scouts so he ended up being tent-mates with a creepy reprobate whose name I can't remember. I do remember looking over at his tent and seeing Michael sitting on his bunk with that guy standing in front of him waving his dick around like a helicopter. I was glad I wasn't in Michael's shoes.

Across the way from our tent, Michael's older brother Bobby and another boy from the neighborhood, Johnny Stottlemyer, were setting up camp. Jay and I went over to see how they were settling in, and for some reason, maybe it was because I had seen that creepy reprobate waving his dick in front of Michael Hunter's face, or maybe I just wanted to see what I could get away with, I started shouting, "We want a show! We want a show!" as if Bobby Hunter and Johnny Stottlemyer were a couple of strippers and Jay and I were some dirty old men. I don't know how I knew about such things, maybe I saw something somewhere on TV or maybe it harkened back to Kim Bell's go-go boots, but I knew that if I said the right thing I'd get those boys out of their clothes. I also had a suspicion that they were old enough to have pubic hair, and I was fascinated by pubic hair, seeing as I had none yet.

"We want a show! We want a show!" Evidently that was the right thing to say because after some coaxing those two thirteen-year-old boys were dancing naked, to my supreme delectation. I don't know what Pink Floyd felt about it all. He might have been a little bit shocked!

Later that night, when the sun had gone down, I slipped out of my tent and crept over to where the older boys were camping, in search of a more private show of my own. They seemed more than willing to give me one. It didn't take nearly as much coaxing this time. I got a lot closer and asked if I could touch their pubic hair. Bobby

Hunter's was soft and downy whereas Johnny Stottlemyer's was black and wiry. I liked Bobby's pubes a lot better. Both of their cocks were hard and I had never touched a hard penis like that before. I was fascinated by the heat and the feeling of the hardness under their skin. I touched them for a while until they began to giggle, then I ran back to my tent, then back to them. It was a game of cat and mouse, me going back and forth, until finally I had enough and decided to go to sleep.

THE NEXT DAY, I VAGUELY RECALL WORKING ON getting some merit badges, one in basket weaving, the other in citizenship. I don't remember my days at Scout camp very clearly, but I know I returned to those boys' tent the next night. Although it seemed very silly, much like a game to me, there was something dangerous and exciting that urged me back there. They were a few years older and seemed much bigger than me, but I felt that I had some sort of power over them. They were very excited, and insistent.

As it turned out, Bobby had a crush on a girl named Alice, so I asked him what he would do if I were Alice, and I told him he had to call me Alice, and imagine that I had boobs and long blond hair. At the time I didn't know any technical terms for anything sexual. I'm not sure he knew much more than I did. He was much more interested in what I might do to him as Alice than what he would do to me.

He started out with instructions like "touch it," "play with it," "hold it," all of which I did. Then he said, "Kiss it." I wasn't about to do that. I was much less interested in Johnny, but felt that I should at least be fair and do the same to Johnny just so he didn't get mad or have his feelings hurt. I had them very worked up, and they were making lots of noise. Finally a Scoutmaster came to their tent to find out what all the fuss was about. I quickly hid under Bobby's cot. When they had calmed down and the Scoutmaster had left, Bobby said, "Blow me, blow me." I had no idea what that meant, so I began to blow on his penis. I blew on it and played with it for a while until he started making low groaning sounds. Then some juice shot out of his dick and got all over my arm and chest. I had no idea what it was, but as soon as it happened, I ran out of the tent and made my way in the dark to a faucet they had in the woods for us to brush our teeth and wash ourselves. I splashed myself with the cool water, but no matter what I did I couldn't get the sticky stuff off of me. It was as if I had walked through a spiderweb. For some reason I was scared. When I got back to my tent, I lay in my sleeping bag in the dark feeling that I had done something wrong, that I had sinned, and I didn't know what to do about it. I remembered that in Sunday school we'd been taught that if we had sinned we had to ask forgiveness from God and the person whom we had sinned against. So I prayed for forgiveness from God, but I couldn't figure out for the life of me whom I'd sinned against.

FOR THE REST OF THE WEEK, JAY, MICHAEL, AND I hung around together, even though I didn't like Michael. He seemed like one of the few people

I could relate to, maybe because I knew he was staying in that tent with that crazy kid flopping his dick in his face. Michael kept repeating this rhyme while we walked through the woods: "Tom, Dick, or Harry, who should I marry? I'll marry Tom because Tom's dick is Harry." We would laugh uproariously.

That stupid poem had tremendous resonance for me because I was only interested in Michael's brother—I wanted to check out his pubic hair. After Bobby came on me I never went back to the tent. I had been overcome by guilt, and I didn't want to get sticky again. The entire experience at Boy Scout camp felt like a test that I had to pass, but I couldn't understand why I had to be there. Even though I was constantly being placed in settings and situations because I was a boy, it never made sense for me to be in them because I never felt like a boy.

I wrote a postcard to my Pop-Pop saying that I was having a good time but that the neighbor boys were teasing me. I never felt judged by my Pop-Pop. I trusted him and felt that I could communicate what I was feeling, having just turned eleven.

When I got home I was still troubled and confused by what I had done in the tent. Part of me wanted to just forget about it, but I was deeply concerned that it was going to cause me to go to hell. My grandfather asked me what I meant when I had written about the boys teasing me. I told him it was nothing. Evidently he had shown the postcard to my mother. My mother asked me about it one day, taking me by surprise. It wasn't something I wanted to discuss with her. Any time I talked about being teased, her only advice was, "You just shake your fist at them and you tell them, 'Bug off creep!'" which obviously wasn't very helpful. And in this case, I certainly didn't want her to take up the issue with the boys. I just wanted to forget about it and pretend that nothing had ever happened.

So I told her it was nothing, but now I was thinking about it even more. The subject had been brought up twice since I had come home. It seemed like my guilt was a rope that was getting tighter and tighter around my neck. Was God watching me? What should I do? I kept thinking about what I'd learned in Sunday school, and even though I'd asked for forgiveness from God I still hadn't come up with a proper answer as to whom I'd sinned against. Finally I thought, "Well my parents wouldn't want me to do that, so I probably sinned against them." I resolved that I was going to tell my mother what had happened.

ONE SUNDAY MORNING WHEN MY MOM WAS GET-ting ready for church, I told her I needed to talk with her about something. In my mind I imagined I would tell her what happened, and she would say it was okay but that I should never do it again. Then she would hug me, and that would be that. I never expected she would react the way that she did.

We were in the dining room, on a sunny June morning. I'd resolved to tell my mother because I needed her to tell me it was okay, that she forgave me, that I wasn't a bad person, and that I wasn't going to hell.

In the past, I had gotten in trouble for getting naked with other kids in the neighborhood and with my cousin Pam, who was the same age as me. When Pam and I got caught in my grandmother's milk house, she was playing a hoochie-coochie dancer doing a striptease and I was cheering her on. My mother came down the path, caught us, and brought us inside, telling us how terrible it was and that we had ruined Sunday dinner. She insisted my father spank me, which he did. My mom was fuming, so angry that she confronted my aunt and seemed completely shocked and appalled that Aunt Sandra refused to spank my cousin. "I'm not going to spank her for that," my aunt said. I could tell that my aunt thought it was funny, which confused me even more.

It wasn't common for me to tell my mother I needed to talk with her about something. My mother could be very funny and had a great ability to make people laugh; at times she could be terrific company. But she had a very conservative streak when it came to sex, and was extremely judgmental of others in general, so I learned very early on to keep my life as compartmentalized as possible in order to avoid her criticism. But I thought that because this was important, and because it was a Sunday morning, she would be kind. Instead, she responded in such a way and with such force that I feel reverberations of her hysteria to this day.

I told her that I got the boys to put on a show for me, that they asked me to play with their penises, and that I had. But I told her that I had asked God to forgive me and that I didn't know what to do now. She became hysterical. It was as if I had completely disappeared. She went into a frenzy and it became all about her. Suddenly, it was as if I was in the middle of a tornado and I became very small. She got on the phone and called both the boys' parents and insisted they come over to the house with their children immediately. The Hunters showed up with Bobby. Mr. Stottlemyer and Johnny arrived not long after. It was like my mother was holding some sort of tribunal.

I sat on the couch curled up in a ball with a pillow in my lap, absolutely mortified. I was frozen, numb. I wanted to disappear. I was forced to tell the story to the boys' parents. My mother spent most of the time arguing with Bobby Hunter, who stood up for himself, saying truthfully that I had initiated everything, which I admitted. But my mother was adamant that because they were older it was their fault. It seemed the main thing for her was that the boys were the guilty parties and that all blame had to be shifted from me onto them. If I was not responsible for what happened—her logic seemed to imply—if it was their fault, it was also the fault of their parents. They had raised reprobates for sons who had taken advantage of my youth, vulnerability, and naïveté. None of this was true, of course, but in her eyes it made them the guilty parties.

I came to realize later that what we were there for really was to put her mind at ease that she was, in fact, a good mother, and that none of this was her fault. She had a hard time having a son like me because I was fun, amusing, good company, doted on her, went shopping with her, helped her pick out shoes, paid attention to her, thought she was beautiful, and yet she knew, and I knew she knew, that inside me there was something different, and she was ambivalent about what she should do about it. She had always been the pretty one in her family. She had married well. She had a beautiful home, a boy and a girl, and everything almost looked just as she wanted it to. Almost, but not quite. The only wild card was me. I was her Achilles' heel. With just a look or a wisecrack her brothers and sisters could let her know that something was wrong with me. She needed to find a way to change me. I was a sissy, and as I got older it became more and more obvious that changing me wasn't going to be easy. In our culture, then and now, everyone blames the mother. I think she took that on. So this ad hoc tribunal brought out into the open a simmering conflict that had been growing for years, and she fought like hell to make sure that both she and I were off the hook.

She won the argument and forced everyone else to admit that they were wrong. The battle she fought was for herself, though, not for me. She won her battle but, without knowing it, she started a war that I would be forced to fight for a long time to come.

After the neighbors had gone, I went to my bedroom and lay down exhausted, yet seemingly absolved of any guilt. My father came into my room and told me that curiosity was normal, and that even though I should never do it again, it was over and I shouldn't feel bad. I was shocked. My father and his reactions were always held up as some sort of veiled threat, that he would be even more unforgiving than my mother was. She would often say, "You better hope your father doesn't hear about this," or "When your father gets home you will really get in trouble." So it didn't occur to me to go to him first instead of to my mother. I was so far removed from him emotionally because he never really shared his thoughts or feelings, and I couldn't relate to that remoteness. He was a stranger to me. But on that June afternoon he told me that everything was going to be okay, and I believed him. But the damage was done.

From that day on I was branded a fag. Bobby Hunter took revenge by spreading the tale far and wide about how I gave him a blow job.

I FOUND OUT HE WAS ANGRY LATER THAT VERY afternoon when I was out for a bike ride. After the conversation I had with my father, I felt as if two tons of concrete had been lifted off of me. I had somehow weathered the tornado my mother had whipped up, and I believed all of this would now be behind me.

I decided to get out of the house to clear my head and enjoy the feeling of liberation. I wasn't going to go to hell after all. I was just a normal boy who had done something that lots of kids do. But when I turned the corner onto Monroe Avenue as I was riding past the Hunters' house, Bobby called me over to their yard, and I knew that it wasn't over yet. He threatened me and told me he was going to ruin my life. I can't say I blamed him. I would have done anything to take back what had happened that morning. I told him I was sorry, but there was nothing I could do after what my mother had said. He was enraged.

I had to ask myself, why did I tell her? It became obvious immediately that I should never have said anything. It was certainly obvious to Bobby Hunter. But in that regard, my mother was right: he was older, and knew better. You don't tell your parents everything. I had just learned that lesson for the first time, and not in the best possible way. It took a while for the full scope of what had happened to really hit me.

DURING THE FIRST WEEK OF MIDDLE SCHOOL, which was the sixth grade, I was in the cafeteria looking for a seat when I heard a boy I didn't know say to another one, "I heard that kid sucked a guy's dick once." I was mortified, not only because they were talking about me and I didn't know them, but because, as I said before, I didn't suck it, I just blew on it. I didn't think that was the right time to correct them, but I realized that if those boys knew about it, a lot of other people did too.

After that I never really knew who knew what where so it made me very paranoid. I could never know when I met anyone for the first time what they already knew about me. I was notorious from the age of eleven onward. That may sound very dramatic, but I'm afraid it's true. Early on

I had described what had happened to my best friend Lesley, because I had never really been able to talk about it with anyone else. I was surprised to hear that she already knew about it. She said that everyone did.

"Your parents know?"

"Yes, that's how I found out. They were talking about it at dinner one night."

If Lesley's parents knew, it stood to reason that everyone's parents knew. A story like that is the kind everybody loves to tell. I was surprised that her parents still let me come over and play with her. My mother wouldn't have. Sometimes I would even spend the night. They weren't as judgmental about what had happened as my own mother had been, so I found a safe harbor there.

The Pearmans had moved into the neighborhood from Virginia the year before. They had Southern accents and seemed very down to earth. Lesley was older than me and I originally became friends with her brother Jed, who was my age, but quickly became friendlier with Lesley. She became my best friend and has remained so for life.

She was very smart and loved to read, and we spent most summer days in her bedroom. The Pearmans had central air-conditioning and kept their house very cold, so I spent most of the summer in shorts wrapped up in a gray alpaca blanket. Lesley's entire bedroom wall was covered with posters of Elton John. I think she liked him because he was bisexual. We were obsessed with Bernie Taupin's lyrics: "Goodbye, Norma Jean . . ." The opening lines of "Candle in the Wind" always made me cry thinking about poor Marilyn overdosing in Hollywood. How could someone that beautiful be so sad, I wondered. Elton John was flamboyantly covered in sequins, feathers, outrageous glasses, platform shoes, and had a hairy chest to boot! He terrified me. He was everything I was supposed to loathe in myself, and everything I was afraid I would become. I knew that I didn't want to be like him, and yet my best friend loved him, and we listened to his music nonstop.

Lesley would sit on her bed, reading the latest Stephen King novel, or any and all science fiction and fantasy novels she could get her hands on. She lived in her world of fantasy and adventure and I lived in mine, reading books about movie stars, biographies of Lauren Bacall, Gloria Swanson, Vivien Leigh. I was obsessed with Tennessee Williams's *A Streetcar Named Desire*, and would often perform Blanche DuBois monologues for Lesley's amusement. I would sing for her too. One night, early into our friendship, I spent the night with her and her brother. My mother was scandalized that we had all slept in the same room, but she would have been even more scandalized if she'd known I'd performed Donny Osmond's hit song "Puppy Love" with my pj's swinging over my head and flying from the top bunk. Lesley loved it.

In those days we were reading a lot of books about autism and children with mental handicaps. I was convinced that if I didn't become a movie star, I would become a teacher of mentally disturbed children, or a therapist. There was no question that Lesley would become a famous writer. We both loved a book called *The Man Without a Face*, which was later made into a

Mel Gibson movie. Lesley was crazy about Mel Gibson because he played a disabled boy named Tim based on a character in one of her favorite books. We had no idea how much of a mental case he would turn out to be off screen. *Dibs in Search of Self* was another one of our favorite books. *Dibs* was the story of an autistic boy. We loved the book because it took us on this young boy's journey of self-discovery and understanding, something both of us lacked. We barely knew ourselves. The only place we could explore was in these books, in Lesley's room.

"Why do you want to spend all of your time in some girl's bedroom?" my mother would ask. "It's not normal. People see you go into that house, and you don't come out for eight hours. Do you spend the whole time in that room?"

I couldn't tell my mother that any place other than home felt safer to me. I wasn't attacked in Lesley's room. I wasn't criticized in Lesley's room. I wasn't a failure as a boy in Lesley's room. I was just myself, whatever that was.

ONCE I ENTERED MIDDLE SCHOOL EVERYTHING changed. I had gone in and out of being popular in elementary school, but I had become confident and comfortable being around the same kids for six years. Middle school was a new set of people altogether. Now I not only had to negotiate the fact that I didn't like boys, but I also knew they didn't like me either, and they had a scurrilous reason not to.

People say that there is an unusually high percentage of queer people with ADD. My theory is that because we know from a very early age that we are different, and because we never really know who the enemy is or who might turn on us at any minute, we become hypervigilant about everything that is going on around us. Perhaps attention deficit disorder is a misnomer; maybe it should be called hyper-attention awareness. It's not that we can't pay attention to anything in specific, it's that we are trying very hard to pay attention to everything in general as a self-defense mechanism.

Around the time I was in sixth grade my cousin Jan, who I looked up to very much, started attending a charismatic Pentecostal church down-town in what had formerly been an old movie theater. Across the street from the church was a coffeehouse for teens called the Fisherman's Net. I thought Jan was very beautiful and cool with her long straight red hair and bell-bottoms. She played guitar and often she took me with her to the Net where we would sing together. Even though I was one of the youngest people I felt very comfortable there.

My assumption was that people who were Christian would be less cruel to me, and I hoped that if people knew that I was a Christian, they would know that what everybody was saying about me wasn't true. Christians don't suck cock. I became a great big Jesus freak and started showing up for the sixth grade with huge crosses hung around my neck. My Aunt Joyce had given me one cross from Israel, which had been carved out of olive wood. Another one had a thick copper chain with a huge filigreed copper cross hanging from it, which I eventually had to stop wearing because it turned my neck green.

I thought that wearing those crosses would protect me and that I could respond to people's comments with righteous Christian indignation and protest my innocence if I had these symbols of Jesus to remind them what I was really all about. I also set out to win over my teachers and became quite an ass-kisser, so that I would at least have people in positions of authority on my side. I tried anything to avoid the catcalls and occasional swats to the back of my head I would receive in the crowded hallways of North Potomac Middle School.

As it turned out, one of my most vocal opponents was none other than Michael Hunter, Bobby's younger brother. He was always shouting "fag" at me or encouraging other people to do it. Our hatred for each other was on display for everyone to see. The irony was that Michael and I had finally started to become friends at Scout Camp, and had become playmates over the course of that summer. But once we got to the new school he used every trick he could to humiliate me. Maybe it was to impress his older brother, maybe it was to impress the other kids, maybe it was to get back at me for being so snotty to him when he first moved into town. Most likely it was because he knew we had something in common and he wanted to make sure no one else would think so, too. One thing is for certain, as horrible as he could be, I was just as good at giving it back to him. I had all the girls on my side.

Although I didn't usually like playing games that boys liked to play, I did have something of a tomboy streak in me. I liked climbing trees, running, playing on the monkey bars, and games of intrigue. This was during the Vietnam War, so we were seeing images of war and violence on the television set every day. One of the games the boys in the neighborhood would play was war. We all had toy guns. The louder and bigger the gun the better. I even had one that shot off sparks. Michael and I were always on opposite teams. One time, he shot me and I refused to die. I said I was only wounded so he took me as a prisoner and dragged me into his garage for questioning. Before I knew it, I had been strip-searched and was up against the cool, concrete wall of the garage with Michael's warm breath on my neck. It was a still, late summer afternoon and outside it was very quiet with the lazy sun hanging overhead; in the garage it was cooler and the smell of gas and cut grass from the nearby lawn mower filled the air. Although he was only a kid, Michael had rough hands from mowing lawns and delivering papers early every morning. Of course we were too young to come, so we just rubbed our naked bodies against one another until my punishment was complete. After that afternoon, I started going to his house more often. One of our favorite games was this very tedious board game called Risk. The ultimate goal was world domination. We would play until it was clear that someone was beginning to take the lead. After conquering Mongolia or Irkutsk, the game pieces would begin shooting through the air at the opponent's crotch and before we knew it, one of us was forced to surrender.

We didn't restrict ourselves to merely playing indoors. When we were in one or the other's home, it could be very dangerous. Several times, we were in his parents' bed when we heard his mother come home and we had to quickly put our clothes on. So quite often we found odd places to meet outdoors, sometimes in very dangerously public spots. Pangborn Elementary School was just down the street and had recessed doorways. Many afternoons we met in the doorways of the school where we couldn't be seen by anyone in the neighborhood. The janitors were still cleaning in the school, but we knew that if we lay down below the windows no one could see us. I don't know how we didn't ruin our clothes, rolling around on the concrete having sex, but we didn't. When it got colder and we needed more protection, we would crawl into the dumpster by the school cafeteria door if it wasn't too full of rotten vegetables or milk cartons. Whether it was full or not, the smell of sour milk permeated the air, so every now and then we'd have to open the door and hope a breeze would come in. We both enjoyed role playing—some might call it psychodrama. My favorite game we played was Captain Kirk and the Alien Seductress. One of us would play Captain Kirk and the other would be a floozy from outer space who would seduce Kirk and tease him to the heights of ecstasy so that he would spill a Starfleet secret.

NO ONE WOULD HAVE KNOWN ANY OF THIS WAS going on if they'd seen our vicious ongoing battle in the hallways of North Potomac Middle School. Perhaps as a foreshadowing of his starring role as Tango on the highway so many years later, Michael loved to assume the role of a police-man who would bust me for an infraction, from suspected prostitution to carrying a concealed weapon. Of course, the fact that I was resisting arrest goes without saying. If I had had a car, perhaps I would have gotten into it and led him on a one-hundred-mile-per-hour car chase like he did to the county police in West Virginia so many years later. My arrest usually led to a very vigorous frisking.

Our prepubescent sex life was dangerous and exciting. This combination of attraction and revulsion was extremely confusing. I really did hate him but there was something irresistible about our ongoing physical relationship. I felt what we were doing was wrong and I'm pretty sure he did too, but between us, we found ways of acting out fantasies and exploring identities we never would have gotten to discover otherwise. It drove me crazy that he still had to assert himself, or I should say impose himself, into my life in other ways by harassing me, teasing me, and calling attention to himself when we were at school. I hated him so much for setting up this dynamic in which he was the tough "straight" boy and I was a faggot at school, while we were both complete sex pigs in private. It didn't seem fair, and I felt powerless to do anything about it.

AT THIS POINT, NO ONE KNEW ABOUT OUR PRIvate encounters. His mother didn't like me because of my earlier encounter with her older son, but she was clueless to all of the activity that was going on under her nose. Sometimes we would be in his swimming pool while his mother was in the kitchen cooking and one of us would be below the surface giving the other a blow job. In winter we would build snow forts high enough so that my mother couldn't see us from behind her kitchen counter. As she washed the dishes we would be out in the freezing weather in a sixty-nine position, just out of sight. In the summer we would climb up in trees and, concealed by the foliage, give each other blow jobs. As all this was happening, the changes in our bodies were evident as well. I remember when Michael got his first pubic hair, which was a few months before I got mine. We were both very excited. He felt like he was a man, which was very important to him. As he strutted around flaunting his pubic hair, I put on my mother's bra and danced around the living room. One day, we heard my mom arrive home from the grocery store. We put on our clothes and ran out to help her bring in the groceries and damned if he didn't tell her that I had been wearing her bra. This was the kind of thing that drove me crazy. Why did he have to tell my mother that I was wearing her bra? It reinforced everything that she hated about me, got me in trouble, and made the rest of my day miserable while he went off smug and self-satisfied.

Of course there was no logic or reason behind what we did. Our bodies were surging with desire and a carnal drive that overrode any rational thought. As soon as one of us got the urge, the other one was there. Sometimes on summer nights I'd hear him scratching at my screen window, and I'd raise the screen and stick my cock out the window for him to suck. It was a good thing he was on the second floor and there was no way I could get to his window or I would have probably broken my neck trying to do the same thing. As soon as he disappeared, my disgust would always return.

IN RETROSPECT I IMAGINE WE WERE BOTH JEALous of each other. Michael had a tremendous ease with adults, and my mother seemed to like him very much. He was, in her eyes, a "go-getter." He had a paper route and when we had been in Cub Scouts, he would go door to door selling things, making money for the troop. He mowed lawns for extra cash, and was sassy in a way that was funny to some people. And he was a flirt, which can be cute in children sometimes. I, on the other hand, was no longer my mother's most glamorous accessory. I was, in her words, a "siss-biscuit."

"Don't be such a siss-biscuit," she would say. I was happy being thought of as a sissy, but I considered myself to be more of a tomboy because I liked climbing trees. I didn't like sports and was certain I had been born in the wrong body. I didn't want to mow lawns or have a paper route. I liked babysitting and taking care of people. My parents forced me to mow people's lawns for cash and when I spent my money on *Vogue* or *Tiger Beat*, they criticized me for wasting it on "that stupid stuff." I didn't see what the point was in making money if I couldn't spend it on what I wanted.

"Why can't you be more like Michael Hunter?" was probably the worst thing my mother could have said to me and maybe she knew it. I've asked her about it since then and she claims she doesn't remember saying it.

Sometimes I justified my sexual liaisons with Michael by telling myself that if I had sex with him he would be more likely to leave me alone at school. Looking back I realize having sex with him might have encouraged him to treat me even worse.

ONE SUMMER, SEVERAL OF THE OTHER BOYS IN the neighborhood and I decided to make a tree house in the woods. In spite of the fact that I was a known faggot, the other boys either didn't care or thought they knew better because we had all grown up together. I passed a zillion sissy tests to prove how tough I was—jumping off this, riding my bike over that, setting fire to something else. Perhaps they were even titillated by the idea of my being a cock sucker. In any case, they never gave me any shit about it. Not far from our neighborhood, there was a plant that manufactured rubber products and behind it were huge stacks of wooden pallets with piles of rubber mats on them. We dragged a bunch of the pallets through the woods and constructed ourselves a tri-level tree house that you could stand up in, with a roof. We decided to line our tree house with the rubber mats to keep the cold weather out, so we nailed them inside and outside the pallets with about three inches in between for insulation. Our tree house had a door and a window, a mattress and a cooler. Once finished, it became Michael's and my regular spot for after-school sex.

One day, when we were thirteen, Michael was hit by a car and broke his leg. Going up to the tree house became impossible. I would have to visit him at his house, a place I generally avoided due to the tension with his older brother. Although I wasn't exactly his mother's favorite person in the world, she seemed to be softening to me, as I was the only one of Michael's friends who came to visit him on a regular basis when, due to his crutches, he was unable to pursue his Dudley Do-Right lifestyle of delivering papers, mowing lawns, and all the other activities that made him shine so brightly in the eyes of the neighborhood adults. His mother thought it was nice that I would come and keep him company. He would make himself comfortable on a beanbag chair in the TV room with his leg elevated and I would sometimes give him blow jobs when he was in that position, making sure that I was positioned in just the right spot so that I could lean on his leg and make him scream in pain while I was sucking his dick, just so he knew who was in charge.

In the evening his parents were usually in the TV room, so we would go up to Michael's room and do "homework." It was a Sunday night and Michael was in bed with his leg on a cushion. He had just gotten a new Sonny and Cher record and we struck a deal that I would suck him for ten minutes and then he had to suck me for ten minutes while we listened to side one. He had gotten a new digital clock for Christmas and it was right by his bed. Trust me when I tell you I had my mouth on his cock and my eyes on the clock. As soon as my ten minutes were up I took a standing position next to his bed because his leg wouldn't bend and I was six minutes into my blow job when I heard a rustling in the hallway and there stood Evelyn Hunter with a look of shock and rage such as I'd never seen. Her teased and frosted hair went paler in the dark shadows of the hallway and her voice bellowed out, "What are you doing!? No . . . I don't want to know. Get out! Get out!" She became hysterical, and told me to never set foot in her house again. She screamed at me as I zipped up my pants, "I should call your mother right now!"

"Don't call my mother!"

"Well, will you tell her what happened?"

"Yes, I'll tell her as soon as I get home."

"And you tell her that this time it was your fault, you sick freak!"

"Yes, I will," I replied in tears. "Just don't call her. I'll tell her, I promise."

Mrs. Hunter had no reason to doubt me as I had already confessed to having sex with her other son a few years earlier. As I rode my bike home in the cool fall air, it suddenly occurred to me that I didn't need to tell my mother anything. I thought, what's Mrs. Hunter going to say? "I caught my son sucking your son's dick." I didn't think she would do that even though I almost wished she would. This was a very liberating moment. I'd been honest with my mother and

hoped for understanding once before and as far as I was concerned she had ruined my life with her hysterical response. If I hadn't been honest with her then, I wouldn't be in this jam I was in now, so I resolved to keep this latest development to myself. Once again, I was riding off into the future feeling like the worst was behind me. I also resolved never to have sex with Michael Hunter again, but of course, I did.

NOW THAT I WAS NO LONGER ALLOWED TO GO into the Hunters' house or call Michael on the phone, the only way we could get together was if one of us saw the other riding his bike outside the window at home. I'm sure both of us had very good calf muscles from riding around and around, trying to get the other's attention. As soon as one of us would see the other out of our living room window we'd raise our hand to signify that we'd be in the tree house in five or ten minutes.

By the time we were in eighth grade we were both maturing physically and had been lovers for nearly two years. In the summertime that rubber-lined tree house could get really hot and sticky. Even though we had a window and a door, we didn't have much ventilation. The smell of the warm rubber could be overwhelming, but we got used to it. Usually we would make out first, and most of our sex consisted of frottage, blow jobs, and the occasional hand job. One time when we were in the tree house Michael was on top of me and grabbed me by the throat very roughly. He looked into my eyes and said, "I could kill you if I wanted to."

Our cocks were hard against each other and a layer of salty sweat had formed between our bodies. The woods around us were silent and still. His rough hand was beginning to choke me and I looked back at him, staring directly into his eyes. Feeling his grip tighten around my larynx, I rasped, "I know you could, but you won't." We both knew why. What we were doing felt too good to give up. He let go and kissed me hard on the mouth, and we ground each other's bodies until we came.

On one particularly humid summer day, we

were both drenched in sweat and we got the idea to see if his penis would fit in my butt. We didn't know it was fucking; we just wanted to see if it would work. It did. I lost my virginity at the age of thirteen in a rubber-lined tree house to a boy who was one month older than me and who I hated beyond words.

IN ACTUALITY, WE DIDN'T ALWAYS KNOW WHAT we were doing, or at least I didn't. I didn't know I had lost my virginity because I didn't know we were fucking. I knew the desire and the feelings inside me were at times overpowering, but even as I was drawn to him, I was repulsed by his aggressive kissing, the way he thrust his tongue into my mouth and mashed his teeth against mine. He smelled of gasoline and mown grass. I was repulsed by the desire and fear I saw in his eyes, his insistence on rimming me, something I would never do, or so I thought at the time. I thought he was foul, a pig. When we were at school I'd hear him say things to girls like, "Why don't you sit on my face?" I thought he was so disgusting. And I knew that girls hated him too, which made me feel better. It also made me feel like I was in a secret sisterhood, but what the girls didn't know was that I was willing to do all the things he suggested in spite of myself, and I liked it, which made me hate him even more.

He filled me, at times, with repulsion for myself. Often I would go directly from the tree house to the shower, and arrive at the dinner table freshly bathed, flushed and ashamed, making small talk with my family who thought I was being rebellious if I used my fingers to eat directly from the serving bowl instead of spooning the Tater Tots onto my plate first.

Other times we would lie in each other's arms with a tremendous amount of tenderness, and sometimes our kisses were very sweet. I could never really tell if he was actually kissing me or if he was kissing some fantasy that he had made up in his mind in order to make what we were doing more justifiable in his own head. True tenderness or love were two things I couldn't allow myself to recognize at the time. It was part of the deal, part of making it acceptable. Having been told how wrong what we were doing was, we thought there was no other option but to cling to our shame. Part of that shame required tacit disgust with each other. There was no way that we could possibly be friends or be seen as having any sort of affection toward each other, so our hatred remained as strong as our lust. Until that equation changed, nothing else would.

AFTER ABOUT A YEAR OF RUNNING AROUND town with great big crosses strung around my neck, and having discovered that I really didn't like being called a Jesus freak any more than I liked being called a fag, I decided to try a different tactic and became more of a class clown. I hooked up with some loudmouthed trashy girls and started honing my skills at sarcasm and rebelliousness toward authority, which came much easier to me than being a goody-goody. I became a "disciplinary problem." When I wasn't at school or in the tree house, I spent most of my time sequestered in Lesley's bedroom, as far away from the world as I could possibly get.

Lesley was my only confidant, the only person who knew what was going on. Somehow she had a level of detachment that allowed her to be both amused and empathetic to the whole situation. It irked me that she actually liked Michael.

Lesley was going through her own dramas with an abusive father. Her home life was unstable and frightening to her, but unlike me she wasn't able to find escape by going away from her home. She did her best to disappear into it and she, too, felt safer when I was there. When we weren't reading or listening to music, we were plotting how the hell we would get out of town. We both found the real world to be tremendously exhausting.

When Lesley's family moved into the neighborhood they started a library promotionals company out of their basement. Her father was a very striking man with a beard and stood over six feet tall. He was an intimidating and articulate person who would regale us at the dinner table with tales of his youth in the mountains of Virginia, while we ate the delicious southern cooking Lesley's mother was famous for. Helen Pearman was prematurely gray, also from West Virginia, and in her way, the backbone of the family. The Pearmans had lived on a farm near Richmond before they moved to Hagerstown, so Lesley, her younger brother Jed, and her older sister Nancy spent most of their childhood in the backwoods and had very strong Southern accents, which I found to be incredibly appealing. It was a difficult adjustment for Lesley to go from the relative freedom of having space and nature to the confines of a suburban split-level ranch house. She was shy and withdrawn, but I was able to make her laugh. Even then I had an irreverent sense of humor and so did she. Her family was not religious so when I first met her I spent a lot of time trying to bring her to Jesus, which I think she enjoyed because she took it as a joke. The philosophical discussions we got into were exotic and new to me.

Nancy, her older sister (I say sister even though she was actually her adopted cousin who lived with the family), had terrible fights with Lesley's father, which often resulted in physical violence. Evidently Nancy's mother had been pretty wild and Mr. Pearman was determined that Nancy would not end up like her. He was brutally strict with both her and Lesley. I rarely saw the full extent of his temper being unleashed on them, but I heard about it and was terribly aware of the skittishness and moodiness that it brought out in Lesley.

This was the early '70s when there were lots of TV movies and books about girls who were mentally unstable. To this day, one of my favorite genres of movie is solitary-girl-in-mental-institution with flashback narrative-catharsis-slow recovery to freedom. I loved books like *I Never Promised You a Rose Garden* and *Sarah T: Portrait of a Teenage Alcoholic* which was made into a movie starring Linda Blair of *Exorcist* fame. One of my favorite TV movies of that era starred Sally Field as a troubled teenage drug addict in Los Angeles who hid a shoe box filled with multicolored pills under her bed, and who dove into a pool during one of her parents' cocktail parties, nearly drowned, and ended up in rehab.

Lesley, too, had a shoe box full of pills under her bed. Although I was very impressed by it, I never took it seriously. As far as I was concerned, we were both inhabiting our own individual narratives along with our joint one within the four walls of her bedroom, a fantasia of stuffed animals and books, furnished with a yellow French Provincial bedroom suite. I don't think Lesley would have picked it for herself and if her bedroom didn't suit *her* personality, mine was an abomination. One weekend I went to stay with my mom's parents out on their farm and when I got home, my mother had redecorated my room in a colonial style, with a navy blue rag rug and curtains with cowboys and Indians on them. On the walls were James McNeill Whistler prints of cavalry soldiers and American Indians on horses with guns and bows and arrows. There was a toy box with rough ropes as handles. I took one look at my new room and burst into tears. My mother, who seemed quite proud of her handiwork, was shocked by my reaction. Who was this room for? Certainly not me. Never in my life had I ever expressed admiration for cowboys or Indians. I had been on a pony ride or two in my life and enjoyed books about horses, like *National Vel-*

vet, *Black Beauty*, and *Misty of Chicoteague*, the story of a wild pony who swam from Chicoteague Island to the mainland to be tamed by a loving family. But none of these books were based on ideas of manifest destiny. Looking back on it, I can see how that philosophy was being played out in our home as my parents attempted to push my spirit deeper and deeper into that toy box.

I DIDN'T TAKE LESLEY'S BOX OF PILLS VERY SERIously, I guess, because we were both free to explore any narrative we desired and place ourselves as the main character in any story we wanted to write for ourselves. I prayed every night that I would wake up the next day and be a woman, and in Lesley's room I was allowed to be one. But I also knew that when I left the room I would still be seen in whatever way the adults around me chose to see me. Although I got angry and frustrated by that, I accepted it as something I was powerless to change. I didn't realize that Lesley was in actuality more desperate than I was.

One day I called to see if she was awake so I could go over and see her, as I did every day. Her mother told me Lesley was ill, but she could talk to me for a minute. When Lesley got on the phone she told me that she had just gotten back from the hospital because the night before she had taken all the pills in her shoe box in an attempt to kill herself. She had to have her stomach pumped. I froze.

"I'll be right there," I said, and slammed down the phone. It took me a few minutes to get dressed and collect myself. I was absolutely shocked and horrified at the idea that I could have lost my best friend. I didn't know what I would do without her, and I didn't know what to say, but I made my way quickly to her house, walked in the door and down the steps to the family room where she was sitting on the couch wrapped in a blanket. I was in such a state that I was shaking. All I could manage to get out was, "If you ever, EVER do that to me again, I'll fucking kill you myself!" I was so angry at her. Even though I saw the sadness and tears in her eyes, I couldn't control myself. I didn't know what to do. I turned back around and ran out the door. We didn't discuss it again until much later, when I told her how terrible I felt for being so cruel and insensitive during such a horrible time for her, but she told me that my reaction had been so bold and heartfelt, and the expression on my face had been so brokenhearted and full of pain that, in fact, it had been the best possible thing I could have done. It let her know how deeply I loved her, and that her life was valued. It gave her courage to go on. It wasn't the end of her problems, though. In a short time, she was sent away to live with her aunt and uncle in Ohio, and I didn't see her again for quite some time.

WHILE SHE WAS AWAY, I HAULED ALL OF HER stuffed animals—a huge bear, a giraffe, and a tiger, along with dozens of others, some of which were at least three feet tall—to my house. I thought that somehow by bringing her energy into my room I would be able to recreate our sanctuary in my own home and somehow get by without her. It didn't work. No matter what I put in there

I never felt comfortable. Before she'd gone away to the hospital, we had decided we were going to run away from home and stay with her sister, who had by now graduated from high school and gotten out of town. But Lesley couldn't wait and I was left to my own devices.

One afternoon, I went to a pool party held by one of my mom's coworkers for the ladies and their kids. I loved swimming and was always very impressed by anyone who had a pool. In fact, Michael Hunter's mother said that I was "using Michael" and pretending he was my friend so that I could swim in their pool. Of course at the time she didn't know that while I was using him, I was sometimes submerged in the water, sucking his dick. Parents have no idea about the deals kids make with each other, and how wrong they can actually be.

During the pool party at Ms. Nestor's house, I heard one of the "girls from work" mention to my mother that she had seen in the newspaper that the local community theater group, the Potomac Playmakers, was holding auditions for *The Sound of Music* and was looking for kids to play the Von Trapp children. I immediately started pleading with my mother to let me audition. I was afraid she would say no, just as she had said no to ballet and piano lessons, but to my surprise she said yes. Before I knew it I was at the Women's Club on Prospect Street singing "Who Will Buy" from *Oliver*. I was cast as Kurt, the youngest Von Trapp.

I immediately developed a kinship with the other actors playing the Von Trapp children, who were from other parts of the county. I knew I was good at what I was doing. One of the girls who was playing Marta, a girl named Carrie Whitely, and I developed a crush on each other, which all the other brothers and sisters thought was funny. My older brother in the show, who later turned out to be gay as well, dared me to kiss Carrie for five seconds, and said that if I did he would give me a dollar. Since kissing her was something I wanted to do anyway, I said I would.

The first dollar I ever earned was when I was five years old with family in St. Petersburg, Florida, visiting my father's aunt and her companion, a man by the name of Mr. Wick. I was very chatty and precocious, full of questions and a running commentary on everything. Mr Wick offered me a quarter to be quiet for one minute. As this was something I did not want to do, and wasn't even sure I could do, I demanded a dollar, which I got.

The dollar from Bobby Higgerman, a.k.a. Friedrich, was one I looked forward to earning. Carrie and I, although we weren't really boyfriend and girlfriend, remained close for many years. In high school both of us decided we wanted to be good at sex so we practiced with each other. Having seen Patti LuPone in *Evita*, Carrie wanted to be able to manipulate men with the power of her fierce pussy just as Eva Peron had done. So we helped each other develop our sexual techniques.

I never knew how Michael Hunter really felt about me but sometimes he did silly things that could have been considered wildly romantic. When he discovered I had this girlfriend, his first move was to try to get her to be *his* girlfriend. Clearly he was more of a man than I was, but that didn't work because Carrie, like most of the other girls, found him to be repulsive. Then he managed to dislodge a stop sign from the street corner and plant it smack dab in the middle of her front yard, a not so subtle hint to STOP. Several years later after I broke up with him and had been ignoring him for some time, we were having a family picnic in my parents' backyard and all the relatives were over. He decided that this was the day he was going to set off the fireworks he'd been saving up for a long time. The next morning, after the picnic, we woke up to discover that he had spray-painted Z's on all the trunks of the trees in our backyard. I never asked him why, but I assumed it was to assert himself and leave his mark—the mark of Zorro. My parents just couldn't understand, but it was all very clear to me. But I'm getting ahead of myself.

WHEN I WAS IN EIGHTH GRADE THE GUIDANCE counselor at our middle school called me in because my teachers were worried. My grades were slipping and I was causing a lot of trouble. I think I was angry, and I released my anger through humor, sarcasm, my constant need to laugh and make other people laugh. The guid-

ance counselor suggested to my parents that we see a child psychologist. My father worked at the health department so he was able to arrange, through one of his colleagues, for us to see a county psychologist for three dollars a session. I think my parents were embarrassed. At that time, no one in my family had ever been to a mental health specialist.

The health department was very close to our school. In one of the sessions I explained to my parents and the psychologist that part of the reason why I was so angry was that I was constantly being harassed and being called a fag and that I didn't feel safe in the school. Sometimes people in the hallway would slap me on the back of the head. I never knew when or what was going to trigger an outburst, and that was why I hated school. I thought that no one was going to protect me, and I couldn't protect myself.

The next week the psychologist told my parents and me that she had secretly trailed me through the hallways and I seemed to be very happy, well adjusted, and popular. She didn't know where this story of harassment was coming from but she had not seen proof of it, although she had only been in my school for a short time. My parents were relieved to be able to think that, in fact, I was fine, and for some reason I was making all of this up. Now I was not only paranoid about who knew what about me, but I was also perceived as a liar, which I wasn't. My experiences and the stresses that I was facing had been completely invalidated.

My gym teacher knew it was true because I cut gym class every day and went to the cafeteria to read instead. Although we never mentioned it, there was a tacit understanding between us that he wouldn't say anything if I wouldn't because he knew that my presence on the field or in the locker room caused quite a sensation, distracted the other boys, and put me in danger. It was easier to sweep me under the rug and I was grateful to be there.

IN MIDDLE SCHOOL WE TRAVELED TO DIFFERENT classrooms for different periods of time but our classmates remained the same. Gym class took place right before lunch. After lunch we had math class with Ms. Maletzky. Toni Mosner, one of the girls in my class, lived nearby and always went home for lunch. One day in the early fall, she got back to school late. She apologized and told Ms. Maletzky, who also lived in the neighborhood, that her mother had to call the police and an ambulance because there was a homeless man in the street across from her house and they thought he was dead.

Ms. Maletzky was shocked, as was I. It was strange that there would be a homeless man in our neighborhood which, although not an upscale one, was a nice area with wide streets and beautiful old trees. When I got home from school I found out that it was not a homeless man; it was actually my Pop-Pop. He had been out for an afternoon walk and had fallen. We rushed quickly to the hospital. He seemed to be okay but was complaining of a terrible headache. Later that night he died of a cerebral hematoma. When I got back to school two days later I explained to Toni that the man was not homeless, but had in fact been my grandfather. I asked her to thank her mother for calling the hospital. Toni was very sad that my grandfather had died, as was I. Pop-Pop was the first person I'd ever been close to who died. My grandmother had died when I was so young I never really knew her. The only things I knew about her were how beautiful her clothes were because I had dressed up in them when I was younger, and I remember seeing the pink suit she was buried in when I kissed her goodbye as she lay in her casket at the viewing. After Pop-Pop's death, my parents and his son Tom went through all of his and my grandmother's possessions, taking what they wanted. In the attic was an old antique bed frame that hadn't been used in years, which had been in the family since the eighteen hundreds. I asked if I could have the bed frame and it was given to me. We had a huge yard sale and got rid of the rest.

When Pop-Pop died, I was sad but I didn't really feel much. It wasn't until one night six months later when I was lying in that bed that I realized I would never see him again and I burst into tears, sobbing so loudly both of my parents came running into my room to see what was wrong. All I could manage to get out was, "I miss him," through heaving sobs. I'd never cried so hard in my life. I also spent a lot of time thinking about what my Christian cousins told me after his funeral: "Your Pop-Pop did not accept Jesus as his personal savior before he died so no matter how kind and how good of a person you think he was, he is not going to heaven." I refused to accept that Pop-Pop's fate was to burn in hell for eternity. Suddenly, all of these so-called good people around me started to look very shabby.

I KNEW THAT IF I MENTIONED ANYTHING ABOUT religion to the lady psychologist or if it became in any way evident to my parents that she had even the slightest anti-Christian views we would never see her again. For my parents it was enough of a challenge that we were going in the first place, but if seeing a psychologist led me to challenge our basic beliefs, it would be over.

I wanted to continue to see the lady psychologist for a while longer. I liked her. She was young and cool and allowed me to talk about my feelings. Sometimes I would see her alone and sometimes with my parents. During one of our private sessions, I mentioned the fact that I was afraid I might be gay. I told her a little about my relationship with Michael and that I didn't want to continue with it. She said that lots of young people experiment and it didn't necessarily make them gay. I was relieved to hear this although I was also afraid that it wasn't true.

The following week I told her that I had thought about what she had been saying. I agreed that it was a phase, and I was not going to see Michael anymore. We never talked about him again but she did say one thing to me that was helpful, something that made every cent of the three dollars an hour she got worth it. She told me that because my parents were willing to put me through college, if I studied hard and was able to graduate from high school with decent grades, I would be able to choose a school any-where I wanted and get out of town. I would dis-cover that there were other people like me out in the world, and I would find a place where I belonged. Being stuck in Hagerstown would be a great tragedy.

I knew she was right, so I resolved that I would somehow get through high school and as soon as I did I would get the hell out of there.

THE SUMMER BETWEEN EIGHTH AND NINTH grade, while Lesley was away, my father and I began to work on refinishing the bed that I had gotten from Pop-Pop's attic. The old cherrywood had been blackened over the years from many coats of varnish, which had cracked and made the whole thing look like it had been in a fire. Together, we used chemicals to strip it. The varnish remover turned the finish into a stinky, syrupy molasses-like texture which we then scraped off with metal spatulas to reveal the beautiful wood underneath. There was a lovely carved filigree on the headboard, which we delicately cleaned off and polished.

My mother had discouraged me from bringing the headboard home, thinking it would sit in the garage forever just as it sat in my grandfather's attic. But my father and I proved her wrong, ordering a special mattress for the bed which was clearly made for people in the eighteen hundreds who were smaller than we were.

Once we saw how lovely the bed was, my parents finally allowed me to redecorate my room. I started by buying a marble top dresser with a nineteenth-century mirror at an estate sale. My room became full of antiques, a new bookshelf, and finally, I was able to put artwork of my own choosing on my walls. Lesley's stuffed animals went back to her house, and I made my own version of an Elton John wall. Instead of hanging pictures of a bisexual British pop star, I covered my wall with movie posters from the '30s and '40s, and clippings from a cache of movie magazines that I had bought at a yard sale. I replaced the cowboys and Indians with images of Joan Crawford, Vivien Leigh, Greta Garbo, and all my other favorite stars in a carefully curated collage that sent my imagination soaring.

Every night I fell asleep imagining that I would wake up the next morning with a closet full of 1940s evening gowns. I dreamt that the headgear I wore with my braces would fly from my head, my hair would grow into a long chestnut mane, and I would wake up looking like a glamorous goddess of the silver screen. I would walk out the door in my high-heeled shoes, get in the car, and go spring Lesley out of the loony bin so we could begin the lives we had planned for ourselves, somewhere no one could find us.

WHEN I ENTERED HIGH SCHOOL I DISCOVERED that things worked very differently than I had hoped. Instead of becoming the glamorous goddess that I had dreamt about, I worked very hard to become as invisible as I could. I channeled my fantasies into the paintings and drawings I did in art class. I spent hours trying to recreate the faces of my favorite movie stars and models from fashion magazines. I entered my pictures in competitions in the county fair and won several blue ribbons and cash prizes, which I then invested in eight-by-ten-inch glossies of my favorite stars. I had heard of a store in New York City called Cinemabilia. One day I called and very awkwardly asked them to mail me pictures of Greer Garson, Ann Sheridan, and Veronica Lake. Years later I found out that Tom Verlaine of the seminal punk band Television, who frequently performed with the Patti Smith Group, worked at Cinemabilia in the '70s. I sometimes wonder if it was him that I talked to, and I imagine an invisible thread of magic leading me to my future life in New York City.

Unfortunately, Michael Hunter and I had French and English together. Whenever we had a class together, there was constant bickering and tension between us. His name-calling and aggressive verbal abuse were never ending. I responded with what I like to characterize as pithy put-downs. He felt, I guess, that by calling me a fag, he was asserting his masculinity, which was evidently in question for him. He also alienated the girls by making lewd sexual remarks, which unleashed my feminist tirades. He ultimately made himself look like a complete asshole, which I don't think was what he intended. Needless to say, our constant tension was disruptive.

In the spring of 1979 when we were in tenth grade, one of our teachers, Mrs. Swisher, also known as "Swish the Dish," got the bright idea to seat us next to each other. I guess she figured that if we were seated next to each other directly in front of her desk, we would be much less likely to hurl insults across the room, disturbing her English class. I found it completely unnerving sitting next to him because, never one for subtlety, Michael started passing me notes in class trying to arrange dates or assignations, and I did not want to think about that while I was at school. I certainly did not want a paper trail.

Unsure what to do, I decided the best thing would be to write a note to Mrs. Swisher, who was young and seemed relatively cool, and explain my situation and why I shouldn't be forced to sit next to Michael. I can't remember exactly what I wrote, but I do know that she returned the note to me the next day and told me that while reading it she had come across the word "homo-sexual" and stopped there. Homosexuality was nothing she understood or wanted to know any-thing about, and if I had any problems in that area I should talk about it with someone else. I was mortified. I think the reason I trusted her was simply because I thought she was beauti-ful. I was too young and stupid to realize that being pretty did not make you anything more than pretty. A good life lesson.

Even though Mrs. Swisher's homophobic response was less than helpful, one good thing came out of it. She allowed me to change seats so I didn't have to sit next to Michael Hunter any longer.

ONE OF THE THREE-DOLLAR SHRINK'S RECOM-mendations was that I get involved in more activ-ities outside of school, so I convinced my par-ents to allow me to become a candy striper. At this point they were so worried about me and so desperate to get me back on the right track that it was becoming easier to convince them to let me do things that they normally wouldn't allow. I was the first boy candy striper in the organization! Since this was the mid-1970s, and a time for breaking down barriers between what roles men and women could assume, the candy stripers were delighted and decided that in order to make it more palatable for young men to volunteer they would change the name from candy striper to volunteen. I was perfectly okay with candy striper and was, I'll admit, a little sad that I couldn't wear the signature pink and white apron. Instead, I was forced to wear khakis and a white collared shirt.

I enjoyed being a volunteen though because I was surrounded by nothing but nerdy teenage girls and solicitious older women. They were a bunch of do-gooders from various socioeconomic backgrounds who worked at the hospital to cheer people up during their dark times. I worked at the snack bar and the gift shop and volunteered at the pediatric ward, making children laugh. My parents justified allowing me to do something so associated with girls by convincing themselves that it would give me experience and job skills for when I began looking for work the summer after I got my driver's license.

I also loved the work because I got to be with so many eccentric old women. My dad's best friend's mother, Ms. Offutt, lived in a dilapidated mansion in his hometown and we would stay with her sometimes when we visited. In her home I was delighted to be surrounded by dusty chandeliers, always aware of the slight smell of a skunk who would occasionally visit the fox that she kept in a cage in her backyard. She was the richest woman in town so she could get away with just about anything. She would sometimes ride a skateboard down the street to go to the store.

She opened my first savings account for me with a five-dollar passbook. My father often complained about headaches. One day she said to me, "I never have headaches. I think your brain has to be full of too many thoughts to have headaches. You probably don't have headaches either."

I was vaguely insulted but she said it in such

a funny way, I went along with it. She was peroxide blond, and when I was in her presence, so was I.

Another of my favorite kooky old women was Walaka Blumberg, the head of the volunteens. She had been born in Italy and married Mr. Blumberg, a Jew. She had a strong Italian accent and made herself up to look like Gina Lollobrigida, who was known, even then, as the poor man's Sophia Loren. I imagine Wally thought she was giving us Sophia, but we knew better. She was hilarious and taught me how to curse people out in Italian. Working behind the snack bar at the hospital meant dealing with a lot of upset and frustrated people, so we got a kick out of mumbling obscenities in Italian under our breath as we served them their homemade cheese-and-pickle sandwiches on toast, which is different from a toasted cheese sandwich with a pickle. Another funny thing about being one of two boys in the volunteens was that the older women were constantly on guard for any sexual improprieties between us and the other girls. I say "other girls" intentionally to let you know that any improprieties were unlikely unless the altruistic retirees were on the lookout for hints of lesbianism.

ONE OF THE FIRST OUTINGS I WENT ON WITH the voluteens was a kind of getting-to-know-you picnic at the city park. I had just seen *Annie Hall*, the Woody Allen film, because the shrink insisted my dad do something with me of my choosing.

My father was a very sensitive man, but he didn't trust his instincts as a parent. He never really had a father of his own because his parents had divorced when he was only three years old. He had made various attempts to teach me things he felt a father should teach his son. When I was a preschooler he bought me boxing gloves. He would get on his knees so we stood about the same height. He taught me how to throw a punch, and I enjoyed it. But one day my four-year-old self gave him an uppercut to the chin and knocked him out cold. I was terrified. I thought I'd killed my daddy. When he came to,

he thought it was very funny, but after that I was afraid to fight.

He took me fishing and hunting but I absolutely refused to kill anything. When we were fishing he said I couldn't talk or I would scare away the fish; I was definitely not interested in anything that required me to be silent. Sometimes he would come up with good ideas. One day he decided we were going to bake a cake from scratch, which turned out to be delicious.

By the time I entered high school my father and I had a big gulf between us. I think he felt it was his responsibility to turn me into a man and after his failed attempts to teach me baseball, to force me to become a champion swimmer, and many other clashes of wills, a simmering resentment had developed. In order to bridge that divide, the three-dollar psychologist suggested my father spend an evening with me doing something I wanted to do. I chose for us to go to dinner at a restaurant we had been to once before at Coolfont, a resort hotel near Berkeley Springs, West Virginia. The restaurant was in a round building surrounded by trees. It was like eating in a mid-century modern tree house. Since this was a special occasion and I got to do whatever I wanted, I ordered Crab Imperial, a popular dish in Maryland in the '70s made out of crabmeat, mayonnaise, and Old Bay Seasoning, and traditionally baked in a blue crab or scallop shell. I was, and still am, crazy about Old Bay Seasoning, which back then was still manufactured at the harbor in Baltimore. Crab Imperial was something I could only order on very special occasions and generally only at restaurants that specialized in seafood. My father was very particular about where we ate and what we ordered because he worked for the health department and knew which restaurants were clean and which weren't fit to eat in. We couldn't, for instance, eat at the Burger King in the Zayre's Shopping Center on the dual highway because it was filthy. All Chinese restaurants were strictly off limits so as a result I never tasted anything even remotely Chinese until I was in college. Dad was also, being a Marylander, very particular about crab dishes. If he ordered a crab cake you could be guaranteed that the verdict would be in after just one bite: "This has too much filler, it's nothing but bread and celery. They think by adding Old Bay people are going to think it tastes like crab. They're skimpin' on meat trying to save money." My first experience with crab was when I was six years old and Dad and I went to Ocean City for the weekend. He had a friend who had a trailer parked in a campground near the beach, and we went over for a picnic dinner. In those days roadside crab shanties were a dime a dozen and you could get a bushel of blue crabs for less than thirty dollars. Dad taught me how to crack the crabs with a wooden mallet, careful not to smash the shell into the meat, and how to extract the meat from the shell without ripping it apart. The goal was to tear the meat as little as possible so you could get a nice big chunk and dip it in butter before sliding it into your mouth. The crabmeat was sweet and delicious, and the mixture of Old Bay, crabs, cheap beer, and salty sea air remains one of the most intoxicating smells I can think of.

As the adults drank their Pabst Blue Ribbon and ate their crabs, a chubby tan girl who was a little older than me decided I was her doll, a role I was more than happy to play. She ran around in her little blue bikini collecting crab claws and hooking them together to make me a crab-claw necklace. Even though it was made out of briny-smelling crab claws it was nice to be wearing a necklace when no one seemed to mind. I felt glamorous.

After we finished dinner we left Coolfont and headed to the Leitersburg Pike Cinemas to see *Annie Hall*, which had just opened that week. I thought *Annie Hall* was one of the funniest movies I had ever seen. It was my first Woody Allen movie, and I was beguiled by how Diane Keaton managed to exhibit a flighty charm and quirky vulnerability all the while being a total femme top who exerted a tremendous amount of sexual power. Dad said he didn't get it. He didn't like movies made in the '70s. His favorite movie was the 1952 film *Moulin Rouge* in which José Ferrer played Toulouse-Lautrec, an artist whose growth was stunted by a childhood accident and who went on to become a great painter of the underground misfits of fin de siècle Paris. My father was quite fond of oddballs and eccentrics, but he wasn't so sure how to handle having one for a son.

On the day of the volunteens picnic I assumed some of Woody Allen's fatalistic, self-deprecating humor. I was a great mimic, and I was feeling very full of myself. I got the girls laughing hysterically over some monologue or story I was telling them. There was one particular girl named Mary Bowan who really seemed to get my new sense of humor. All of a sudden it occurred to me that I had a terrible crush on her, and I asked her out on a date for the following Saturday.

That week I was so anxious and excited about our date that I lost five pounds, which was a lot for me. Neither of us had our driver's license yet so my mom had to drop me off at her house, and we walked to the movies. Fortunately Mary was a little more aggressive than I. She took my hand and held it through the entire film. I thought she was so beautiful. I can still remember the way she smelled, which got me very very excited. For several weeks we talked to each other on the phone three to five hours a night, driving our parents crazy tying up the phone line, reading our poetry to each other, playing music. I was convinced I was in love.

One day I called into the local radio station and won a free record. I went down to the station to pick up my prize and was given a choice between a recording of a band I'd never heard of or one with a photograph of a beautiful girl with long brown hair, red leg warmers, and jeans. Her name was Kate Bush. When I got home I played the record and it was like nothing I had ever heard before. She was singing about Heathcliff and Kathy from *Wuthering Heights*, a novel by Emily Brontë which I had recently read. I got on the phone that night and played the entire thing for Mary Bowan and we absolutely loved it because she sounded like a witch and we were both fairly sure we were witches, too.

Mary went to St. Maria Goretti, a private Catholic high school. I had tried to convince my parents to send me to Goretti but we couldn't afford it. Mary's parents didn't seem to have any more money than mine did but they were Catholic so I guess they were ready to make that commitment. I was raised to believe that Catholics were going to burn in hell because they worshipped a false idol, namely the pope, who they sometimes made the mistake of placing before God, or on a higher level than Jesus. They were idol worshippers. We were taught that our relationship with Jesus was personal and we didn't need any pope between our mouths and the Lord's ears. Anyway, I thought it was exotic that she was a Catholic heathen. I enjoyed the stories she would tell me about her younger sister, who was evidently quite a slut and liked to make out with everyone. On more than one occasion when I called, there would be reports that her mother was in the attic again. Mrs. Bowan had a setting on her vacuum cleaner which allowed it to blow air out instead of sucking it in. She would fill the cleaner bag with mothballs in order to shoot at squirrels, which climbed up the trees and made their way into the attic. It made me feel like a character out of a J. D. Salinger novel, dating a girl with a crazy mother in a housedress shooting squirrels with mothballs up in the attic window. Her father, on the other hand, was a little more intimidating. He had been a speechwriter for Richard Nixon. It seemed the whole family was afraid of him, including her older brother who was gay and wasn't allowed in their home.

By this time, I was thinking that maybe the psychologist was right, maybe my being gay had been a phase. Time had passed and now I had my driver's license. I could borrow my parents' car and pick Mary up and take her out on dates. I enjoyed making out with her, steaming up the car windows in front of her parents' house late at night. My friend Carrie from the Playmakers had taught me the right moves, so I knew how to bring a girl to orgasm with just my hand, and I was feeling confident and turned on. I felt that maybe my problems were over. I had no desire to be normal, but meeting this eccentric girl who loved poetry and the same music I did, and who clearly enjoyed me physically as I enjoyed her, seemed to herald a new life for me. She was hot. One night she came over to watch TV with me and my family. Mary and I were sitting on the couch covered by an old afghan my grandmother had crocheted, watching TV in the basement. We were in the back of the room, seemingly perfectly still, while my parents and sister were sitting in front of us. Unbeknownst to them she was giving me a hand job underneath the blanket. I came and quickly ran out of the room. She didn't give a shit. I loved her for that.

THE NOTE I GAVE TO MRS. SWISHER WAS MY last attempt to reach out to the adult world for help. I realized I was on my own when it came to dealing with my sexuality. My mom's response had been one of pure hysteria, my psychologist had been passive, and Mrs. Swisher had exhibited borderline contempt. The only thing I could do was to try and control it myself. Mary was a godsend to me. I hate to use that expression now, but at the time I still believed in heaven and hell, and that somehow my actions would lead me to one or the other. If nothing else, our relationship provided an outlet for so many pent-up feelings, creatively, aesthetically, and romantically.

My fear of and desire for Michael Hunter had begun to wane. His words of contempt, which were coming much more frequently and furiously in the classrooms and hallways, were having much less of an effect on me. I was feeling more secure and self-confident. I don't think it was because I had blossomed exactly. I was a gangly sixteen-year-old who stood 5'11" and weighed 125 pounds. Sometimes when I was behind the snack bar at the hospital, the kids who came in for a soda would laugh at me and call me pencil neck. But I knew I had talent as a painter, and I spent a lot of time with the crazy pot-smoking actors in the Potomac Playmakers, who were all older than me and didn't care what I did as long as I made them laugh—something I was very good at.

LESLEY FINALLY GOT BACK FROM OHIO. INSTEAD of going to the high school that I went to, her parents sent her to St. Maria Goretti, the same private Catholic school Mary Bowan attended, so she and Mary got to know each other.

I had always enjoyed the fact that Lesley was taller than me. I had walked around as her side-kick with my elbow propped on her shoulder;

next to her I had always felt safe. After she got back, I discovered that I had grown taller than her, which was a very jarring and unwelcome rite of passage. I began to realize that Lesley was the vulnerable one.

She hadn't tried to kill herself again, but it was very difficult for her to remain in her home. It was decided that she would be institutionalized. She went to Brook Lane Psychiatric Hospital, which fortunately was close to where we lived. Now that I could drive my parents' car I could go visit her.

Brook Lane seemed to me to be a very glamorous place full of troubled teens and crazy grownups. It was in the country and had a stream going through it. Built in the '60s it looked like it could have been the setting for any movie of the week featuring a soon-to-be has-been teenage star like Mackenzie Phillips, Linda Purl, or Kristy McNichol. The jukebox in the game room was constantly blaring the most depressing songs. I remember standing by the ping-pong table with Lesley one day when "Dust in the Wind" by Kansas came on.

> Don't hang on, nothing lasts
> > forever but the earth and sky
> It slips away, and all your money
> > won't another minute buy
> Dust in the wind, all we are is
> > dust in the wind . . .

We both started laughing hysterically. "It's just too much," I said. We laughed until we cried, then went for a walk.

Another time I went to visit Lesley with her parents. We walked into her room and found her smoking. Her father went ape-shit. It was one of the few times that I saw him really go after her. He threw her on the bed, screaming at her, "I hope you die of cancer you stupid bitch!" He screamed at her until he was asked to leave.

She said, "You won't let me kill myself quickly, so I'm doing it the only way I can."

After her parents left and we calmed down, we laughed about that too. It was all so absurd.

One of the girls Lesley and I befriended at Brook Lane was an Indian girl, Sue Suvramanian. We went for a walk by the stream, and as we walked Sue Suvramanian told us about her mother, who she claimed was a very famous psychiatrist and who, according to Sue, was well traveled and had actually been on the airplane during the raid on Entebbe, a hostage rescue mission conducted by the Israeli army in Uganda in 1976, but more importantly, a made-for-TV movie that had been a big ratings hit just a few weeks before. As I said, we were all creating our own narratives, and I was delighted by Sue's and fully accepted her story.

It became clear to me that Sue Suvramanian had taken a shine to me when I met her and Lesley at the Valley Mall on Wednesday night. Every week as a special treat the folks at Brook Lane loaded everyone in a van and took them to the mall for supervised shopping trips. Sue Suvramanian bought me a copy of a Beaux Arts poster at the head shop, which I hung in my room next to a needlepoint of a hummingbird on a gold lurex background with cherry blossoms that Lesley had made for me during her summer at her uncle's house in Ohio. I looked forward to our visits at the psychiatric hospital, and there was something about driving away at the end of each visit that gave me the feeling that I was finally gaining some control over my own life. I had more things to think about than some homophobic dumbass who wanted me to suck his cock a couple times a week and who looked like he was coming apart at the seams.

IN A WAY I WAS LUCKY BECAUSE MY FEARS about my sexuality were less intense than my need to express myself. Somehow I found ways to free myself, if only in my mind, by drawing, writing, making people laugh, and socializing. More and more I was able to leave my parents' world where everything was described as overemotional, where most of my feelings and actions were invalidated, to places where the very things that my parents held against me were celebrated. I don't think Michael had that. He wanted more than anything to be popular, but the way he learned to get attention was through verbal assaults and an ungrounded bravado. People grew weary of him. I know I did.

Things were changing quickly. We both had access to cars, and I found myself making out with him, sitting in the parking lot at the school down the road from our house, which I thought was very dangerous because the last thing I wanted was for anyone to see us together. His brazenness started to border on recklessness. Not only was he being much more vociferous at school and more indiscreet—evidenced by the note in Mrs. Swisher's class—he seemed to be almost desperate.

He would drive by my house, gun his engine, or lay down rubber. Sometimes he would set off firecrackers in his yard. Anything to get my attention. I tried my best to ignore him. Occasionally I would break down and see him, but by now it wasn't desire that was driving me to get together with him; I felt like I had to calm him down like one would when feeding an insistent cat, or taking a dog for a walk. I think in a way I was weaning him and myself from what had become, in my mind, simply a bad habit.

When I was with Mary, although I was playing the role of a boy, I felt more comfortable sexually and more feminine than I ever did with Michael, with whom I actually sometimes played the role of a woman. Being with Mary showed me that there is a big difference between acting like a woman and feeling like one. At the time, all of this was so confusing. I could tell Mary wanted to make love to me, and I knew that I wasn't ready.

ONE THING I WAS CERTAIN OF WAS THAT I HAD to end it with Michael Hunter once and for all. But he was persistent. We met each other a few more times—in the tree house, his car, various places—until finally one day, we were in the school yard. We climbed up a tree and, as he stood on a branch several branches below me and gave me a blow job, I realized that I couldn't do it anymore. I wasn't turned on and I'd had enough.

We climbed down out of the tree, got on our bikes, and before we went our separate ways I let him have it. "Michael, I'm sick of you running around telling everyone that I'm a faggot, that

I'm gay, that I'm some sort of a freak. Meanwhile you go around saying things to girls as if you're some sort of straight guy. You're not. I told you I wanted to stop doing this and yet you keep bothering me, and why is that? Because, like it or not, you are a faggot, and you can't do anything about it. I don't know if you've noticed, but over the last few months I haven't come because I'm not into it anymore. I've grown out of it and there is nothing you can do about it. I'm just not into it anymore.

"I don't want you to ever say anything bad about me again or call me gay or I will tell everyone the truth about you—you are a cock-sucking faggot! You love it! You can't live without it! All this time you've been pestering me and I've had sex with you to shut you up so you'd leave me alone, but I'm not going to do it anymore. You, you are a faggot, not me. And if you don't leave me alone I'm going to tell the world. I'm going to tell the whole world about it so everyone will know Michael Hunter is a FAGGOT."

Michael protested, shouting, "No I'm not. I'm not a faggot!"

"Yes, you are!"

I could see it dawning on him that maybe he was one, and that no one had ever told him before that yes, he was a faggot. I wanted to hurt him. I wanted to make him feel all the pain and confusion that I'd felt for the last few years. I wanted to make sure that he hated himself as much as I hated him, as much as I hated that part of myself. I wanted to take out all the anger and frustration that I'd felt, so I started screaming at the top of my lungs, "Michael Hunter is a faggot! I'm going to tell the world that you're a faggot, you faggot!"

I got on my bike and rode away, screaming at the top of my lungs, and left Michael sobbing in the schoolyard, his figure getting smaller and smaller in the distance as I rode away. I'd never felt such a sense of relief in my life. Nor had I felt as much power. Because even though I wasn't sure whether I was gay or not, I knew that I had hurt him as much as he'd hurt me and I felt completely justified. And I knew I would never be afraid of him again or of what he might say about me.

UP UNTIL THAT POINT MICHAEL HAD MAINTAINED a certain level of popularity with French club, junior varsity football, all kinds of student activities. The following year, he dropped out of everything. He lost all of his confidence while I flourished. I never had sex with Michael Hunter again.

Three months later I broke up with Mary Bowan. It was very strange after five years of sexual satisfaction to go without, but one thing I was sure of was that after Michael Hunter I would never have sex with anyone who didn't love me, which limited my field of sexual partners tremendously. It wasn't until years later that I came to terms with my sexuality, and by then the AIDS crisis was in full swing. So in a way, I sometimes think that if it hadn't been for that relationship, I might have been more promiscuous at a time when it would have been much more dangerous for me. While most of the gay boys in my college class were experimenting sexually I was trying to find love. Most of those boys are dead now.

According to the local newspaper, Michael was arrested out on Highway 81 for impersonating a drug enforcement agent. He was found wearing a bulletproof vest with guns in his car and a card he had made saying he worked for the government. His code name was "Tango." He was arrested and released on $2,500 bail.

The next morning he was discovered doing the same thing again but this time he was charged and held on $35,000 bail. The newspaper said he had been diagnosed with mental illness and bipolar disorder. While on bail he left the country and took a cruise to Bermuda. Upon returning to the States he was put in jail, where he remained through Thanksgiving, Christmas, and New Year's. In January he was tried and remanded to Brook Lane Psychiatric Hospital, the same psychiatric hospital where I had visited Lesley so many times. Hopefully he is getting the help he needs.

Other than his mug shot in the newspaper, I have only seen him once since we left high school.

In the late '90s he was mowing Lesley's mother's lawn for extra cash. I heard through Lesley that after high school he enlisted in the army and was discharged. For a while he lived in his car. There was a certain period where he was going to community churches, preaching, trying to be a minister. During a previous incarceration he'd ended up in the hospital with a broken jaw. Michael has had a rough life. When I read about his latest disaster in the *Herald Mail*, I thought back to the first day we met, when he was telling us all about how his father had provided all the glass for the UN building and trying so hard to make himself sound special. In those days disorders weren't diagnosed in children like they are today. And I realized I could probably see the beginnings of his bipolar disorder. Who could have known back then that his delusions of grandeur would one day lead him to call himself Tango while doing his "heroic work" stopping the drug trade on the highway outside of town?

IN MY MID-FORTIES NOW, AND GRATEFULLY childless, I don't know with any amount of certainty what it's like to grow up in these times. But looking back I realize the amount of pressure that we were under then, and what little resources there were for the issues we were dealing with, made things pretty tough.

Our parents were aspiring toward safe, secure, middle-class normality, which was forged through hard work, steely determination, a tremendous amount of voluntary blindness, and a certain hardness that could be crushing to those of us who were unable to fit into their ideal.

As much as I despised Michael at the time and as difficult as it was for me then, I realize now that because he and I were so different from what our parents had hoped for and what society had expected, we became targets, lightning rods for the dissatisfactions of those around us. We were the victims of people who felt the shifting sands of identity and sexuality, and who were sure that they could manipulate, cajole, and torture their children into being what they thought was necessary for the survival of some kind of misguided social contract that we are all supposed to sign on to.

I still haven't figured out what that social contract was, but not long ago I had a dream and in that dream I was at the same family picnic during which Michael Hunter had set off fireworks and later painted Z's on all the trees. Instead of being in his yard, full of rage and desperate for attention, he was sitting next to me on a blanket, just as any teenage boy would do when sitting next to the person he was in love with. My hair was long; I was still a boy, but I was expressing a femininity that was forbidden to me in my youth. No one was paying us any attention because we were just stupid teenagers. No more, no less interesting than anyone else. No more exciting or exotic than any other healthy high school kids. My parents weren't thinking about what was wrong with or right with me. I was just their child. And in that dream it was the first time I'd ever even begun to imagine what my life could have been like if I'd never experienced trans- or homophobia. It was pretty amazing.

I'm grateful to that dream. It was the first time I ever experienced the feeling of what I now call the "luxury of normality." I can't say I aspire to living that way myself because my life has been a constant series of adjustments and acceptances, but I do hope that a time will come when queer children can be themselves without any questions, able to experience the same dramas, heartaches, and joys that any other kids would have to go through, no more and no less.

Acknowledgments

FIRST OF ALL, I WOULD LIKE TO THANK MY PARents for loving me in the best way they knew how, and for providing me with a very good education, straight teeth, and a deep-seated stubbornness (a.k.a. patience!) that has served me very well throughout my life. Dad, Mom, Carol, Mark, Celia, and Logan: I love you endlessly.

I would also like to extend my gratitude to my lovely traveling companion Nath Ann Carrera, who has my heart and undying love, as do Sammy Jo, Caden Manson, and Jemma Nelson. I owe much happiness and love to Susan DeFelice, Mairamie Thayer, Kathy Hudson, my cousins Pam Calandrelle and Jan Bare, and my girlfriends since infancy: Lori McDowell, Teresa

Garling, and Karen Martin. You ladies, along with so many other friends and relatives, made living in small-town Maryland bearable for me and, by accepting and loving me, allowed me to learn to love myself.

A special thanks to Jacob Breslow and Michael Angelo, who sat with me on my fire escape in New York City typing away over coffee and many cigarettes (don't worry, I've since quit smoking them) during the summer of 2010, or as we called it, 20-femme.

Of course, I would never have even thought of writing this story if it weren't for the encouragement of my editor Amy Scholder, so if you don't like it please blame her not me!

This book is dedicated to the memory of my grandparents Ralph and Irene Thayer, and J.P. and Idella Mose. Blessed be.

Vx, 2011